The Core Assets Of Marketing Revealed

With its Dual Implementation Support System attached – The Cellar

Trisha Patricia Amable   6/22/19   The Right Marketing Technique for your business [playbook]

About the author

Trisha Patricia Amable is the creator, owner and CEO of Girlfridayz Limited founded in July 2015 an Online Marketing Consultancy company based in Camberwell in London.

Girlfridayz Limited is an accredited award-winning marketing consultancy company providing B2B and Startup with the following services Marketing, Business Support, and Backup Administrative Services.

Girlfridayz customer journey overview service buying customer journey is a hybrid-brand multichannel, where expert, specialist award-winning result-orientated services are broken down and rebuilt anew.

This epic expertise mapping in a way that empowers Startup & B2B to grow their business through grasping that the services work closely interlinks with your customer's needs.

Girlfridayz logical cognitive approach world-class dual step-by-step Business Support System for startups and B2B to achieve better sales is linked to an online mentoring system – The Cellar that is linked to this playbook The Core Assets of Marketing With Its Dual Implementation Support System – The Cellar.

This Playbook revolutionizes the marketing book industry because it is the only marketing book that is attached to an online mentoring system. A unique solution to support B2B, startups to grow their business effortlessly using progressive strategies and tactics and learning the foundation of marketing and its application to business.

Girlfridayz Limited CEO has developed several marketing theories that contribute to the marketing industry. These theories are alike the previous marketing theories that other great minds have produced in the 20th century and are widely known worldwide and used by conscientious large businesses to grow their business.

Girlfridayz Limited CEO is an author of several business and marketing e-books, has also written a leadership role-play training course which is a core training for staff, and it is available for B2B to train their staff should they want to become a leader or Startup business owner wanting to learn how to set up their business, learning business acumen. She has written two marketing short self-contained courses. This marketing content can be found in Girlfridayz Limited's online store.

Girlfridayz Limited hybrid system is composed of two main parts linked together, the customer shopping stage and standalone services an easy scalable logical system that our customers and prospects can pick any services or use the standalone services approach solution for clients, prospects, and our website visitors. Our dual system is like going to the supermarket and picking the service that you need.

Written by Trisha Amable – Girlfridayz – Website: https://girlfridayz.com
Girllfridayz number 10358020 girlfriday, girlfridayz[tm] is a registered trademark in the UK

Thank You

I would like to extend my sincere thank you to Steve Hackney who encourage me to develop and create a playbook by informing me that a business needs to create a dual implementation support system.

I would like to extend my sincere thank you to my customers and prospects who unbeknown to their input help me shape the content and direction of this Playbook, which is unique in its composition and different from our competitors and all the playbook that other companies produced because it is a new trend.

I thank myself for the hard work putting in this playbook content and its attached mentoring system – The Cellar to bring to the right audience a product that they can enjoy, learn from, and implement content to their business.

I would like to thank Elon Musk for inspiring me to do better and greater with this simple but true quote "Look at the world around you and try to improve it." Elon Musk and Rori Sutherland , Vice Chairman, Ogilvy for asking someone to develop a behavioural psychological model during one of his talk about behavioural science, psychology and marketing. After seeing the youtube video I developed the behavioural psychological model.

Another proud moment at Girlfridayz book drive.

After sending to Laurence Bacow President of Harvard Business School The Core Assets of Marketing With Its Dual Implementation Support System - The Cellar, he was immensely impressed that he viewed it 43 times and replied after a week:

"Thank you for writing to President Bacow and for sharing a sample of The Core Asset of Marketing With its Dual Implementation Support System - The Cellar. We appreciate your thoughtfulness in calling our attention to your book, and we wish you all the best. Amy Fantasia".

He endorsed our book plus The Cellar in recognition of the amazing innovations found in this book for undergraduates and postgraduates.

 Albert did this $E=MC^2$

 Trisha did this $C=NC^2$

And you do this -----

All the people I encounter have inspired me to write this Playbook and create my Marketing Theories model for you to use and the contents of this book. Reading this book and accessing its attached Cellar will inspire you to do greater in your business or your startup to be one of

2

Written by Trisha Amable – Girlfridayz – Website: https://girlfridayz.com
Girllfridayz number 10358020 girlfriday, girlfridayz[tm] is a registered trademark in the UK

the select few businesses that achieves enormous growth and feed the community they are belonging to for years to come.

I sincerely thank all these people with all my heart because in this life in order to grow you need to meet the right people who help you on your journey and never forget your roosters or where you come from as it shape you to be the person that you are.

Thank you for reading this book the manual and implementing its contents to your business or startup because if you implement repeatedly its content, you'll soon discover that you can improve on it and do your own or even better and be the next famous business that people love, admire and adore.

E=MC2
Albert did this the theory of relativity — Physics

C=NC2
Trisha did this the theory of relativity — Marketing

C means Customers
N means Niche 80% of what you do 20% of people relate to it in any industry.

C means Conversion - 20% of your audience buying your products or services in any industry.

x2 repeated purchases of your products & services by 20% of your audience in any industry.

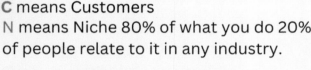

Enhance your MBA or any course that requires you to learn Marketing and its application to business

The Manual for SME

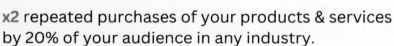

Scan to continue

Figure 1- Lead Magnet to sales this very book you are reading to the right audience

$C = NC^2$ where N is 20% of your market in your industry, C is your conversion and only 20% of your audience buying your products or services in your market and x2 is repeated purchase of your products or services within your audience, market and industry. Therefore the theory of Customers Acquisition created on 4th February 2023 by Trisha Amable CEO of Girlfridayz found that $C = NC^2$ is relative equivalent, hence, $C = NC^2$ is the theory of relativity in marketing and its application to business.

Written by Trisha Amable – Girlfridayz – Website: https://girlfridayz.com
Girllfridayz number 10358020 girlfriday, girlfridayz[tm] is a registered trademark in the UK

Contents

Written by Trisha Amable – Girlfridayz – Website: https://girlfridayz.com
Girllfridayz number 10358020 girlfriday, girlfridayz[tm] is a registered trademark in the UK

Introduction

Let define what is the Core Assets of Marketing. The Core Assets of marketing are a set of tactics used in marketing for centuries and businesses have used them repeatedly to achieve massive success in their businesses and grow their businesses exponentially.

These timeless techniques which are called tactics in marketing are considered by many a well-safeguarded secret that is only given to a handful of people and the selected few who were serious about growing their businesses and becoming huge and well-known enterprises for years to come.

These businesses generated massive profits years by years and achieved unprecedented notoriety Worldwide just by using the Core Assets daily to market, and position their brand as an authority in their industry or across multiple industries.

Why I am sharing this with you it is because the Core Assets do not only apply to a selected few but to every business across the world. The Core Assets do not discriminate against anybody running a business in any industry, and any business can use them to its advantage. It does not care if you are self-employed, an SME or a large business as everybody can use them daily as part of their arsenal which is a pre-requisite for growth and profitability.

Overview

This book is a step-by-step playbook detailing the Core Assets used with a strategy and as far as possible includes practical examples to help see how to combine strategies and tactics to grow your business exponentially with the formula and to achieve maximum profitability over time and get clients for free without spending huge amounts of money promoting your business.

I guarantee you that if you use the Core Assets combined with strategies daily and make it a new habit you will achieve massive growth in your business over time. By practising using the Core Assets with your strategies daily and testing the market to see which combination work best as the Core Assets work and using them rightly you will get excellent result exceeding your expectation.

The value and benefit you get by using the Core Assets and strategies daily helps you acquire knowledge and skills that you can use repeatedly as when you find the strategies which work best for your business you need to systemize it and it becomes part of your business processes because to grow a business need system in place.

It is important to use and implement the Core Assets and strategies together for the best result as without strategies the Core Assets will work but bring you poor results and a strategy without the Core Assets will not get you any results and your business will remain unchanged.

This Playbook includes our contributions to marketing as a whole our novelty and innovation and is copyrighted and registered trademark part of our trademark business name therefore

5

Written by Trisha Amable – Girlfridayz – Website: https://girlfridayz.com
Girllfridayz number 10358020 girlfriday, girlfridayz^{tm} is a registered trademark in the UK

cannot be copied, distributed, rented, lending copies of our models, method and analysis or making an exact adaption of our work and putting it on the internet or any other publication as yours, notwithstanding but including The Cellar membership Dual Implementation Support System model and its access password to anyone.

No part of this publication may be reproduced in any form or by any means, electronic, mechanical, photocopying, recording or otherwise without the prior consent of the author and the publisher.

Distributed exclusively throughout the United Kingdom by Girlfridayz Limited marketing online company.

You need our express consent to use for your benefit and this consent is given to you the buyer of this Playbook to improve your business if you need to mention our models you will need to mention our company name and owner creator of these models including its date of creation.

Which are listed below:

Customers Acquisition method: Girlfridayz Star Sales Principal®© - Deliver your product or service like a seasoned pro created on the 13^h of April 2019 by Patricia Amable CEO of Girlfridayz Limited

Competitor Analysis: Girlfridayz Road Block Competitor Analysis Model®© created on the 27th of June 2018 by Patricia Amable CEO of Girlfridayz Limited

Distribution omnichannel: Girlfridayz Service Catalogue©® online distribution with targeted links can be adapted to product distribution created on the 5th of September 2019 by Patricia Amable CEO of Girlfridayz Limited

GAP Analysis: Gap Reduction Strategic Action Model®© – Your own resistance to change created on the 6th of April 2019 by Patricia Amable CEO of Girlfridayz Limited

Girlfridayz TIME Matrix®© – When it comes to qualifying leads – Remember it's about time. Created on the 13th of April 2021, by Patricia Amable CEO of Girlfridayz Limited. A **strategic planning tool** that can help you to prepare and respond to external influence to retain customers or acquire new customers.

Dual Implementation Support System for the playbook: The world's first dual implementation support system attached to a marketing & business book®© - The Cellar is a how-to guide implementation dual support system attached to this playbook a scalable tangible implementation support system to encourage small business owners to achieve greater and grow their business 10 times folds. Created on Thursday 9th July 2020 by Patricia Amable CEO of Girlfridayz Limited.

Written by Trisha Amable – Girlfridayz – Website: https://girlfridayz.com
Girllfridayz number 10358020 girlfriday, girlfridayz^{tm} is a registered trademark in the UK

Our innovative idea revolutionized the way a marketing & business book can be used and support people, who need prompt and prop to learn from a book.

Our concept is unique because no marketing & business book comes with a dual implementation support system attached to it. We have built the finest dual implementation support system a scalable solution result orientated through a cognitive approach mix for playbook users worldwide.

We believe at Girlfridayz The Cellar to be the best logical cognitive approach world-class state-of-the-art Dual Implementation Support System for the playbook user to encourage business owners using the information in this playbook which contains legacy systems that are worth 10k to you and we guarantee if you implement the playbook information your business will grow 10 times folds.

Discover these great new dominant framework marketing strategies, models, and analysis to acquire prospects and customers over time to help you set business goals and defined your purpose in business, and help with business awareness and business retention.

Should you want to use our strategical dominant framework marketing models; you will find how to use them in this playbook, our new competitor model analysis you will find how to use it and there is a practical example in this playbook, we encourage in this playbook to use our concept of a service catalogue for online distributions and our idea can be adapted to products, see how in this playbook, and download our service catalogue.

Our Gap Reduction Strategic Action Model is a marketing prompt to help you develop an idea using it we develop our Girlfridayz Service catalogue®© by using our model and saw that in term of distribution we could bring the product catalogue concept to service only and bring it as an online application to be downloaded on people computer and all targeted link inserted are clickable back to the pertaining page on our website.

It works similarly to a printed catalogue but for services and the services offered can be displayed on a catalogue and add an order form, vouchers to entice people to purchase services and after you finish designing it and adding all target links to your website services pertaining pages you create a PDF version and offer it as a download.

The TIME Matrix Strategic Model®© – helps businesses to prepare and respond to external influences to retain or acquire new customers. This dominant framework model was created on 13th April 2021.

The 5 Sales Drivers Audience Attraction – Sales Drivers Matrix®© was created on 22nd March 2022 to support small businesses by targeting the right audience with the right message and emphasizing its effect using the 4 complementary Sales Drivers (Guarantee, Call To Action, Irresistible Offer and Social Proof) to achieve sales and increase profitability.

The leads and sales strategic matrix®© dominant framework have been created on 31st March 2022 to respond to the ongoing crisis faces by small businesses and startups since the

7

birth of the social media platforms — Targeting the wrong audience for their products or services, hence the leads and sales strategic matrix highlight that it is essential to speak to the right audience to increase leads and sales.

Girlfridayz Audience Attraction Matrix Complete®© and **Girlfridayz 4 Sales Drivers Audience Attraction Complementary Sales Drivers Matrix**®© were developed on 20-04-22 because small businesses use the Core Assets upside down across the board these days. These dominant frameworks will support you understand that without talking to the right audience you cannot begin to market your business.

You first need to speak to the right person in your industry, then use the strategies and tactics to engage your leads or customers in your content through any channels to eventually purchase a product or service and if they love the product or service and find that it answers their needs and provide a solution to their problem they may grace you with a review and refer you left right and centre and even become your advocate.

Discover these great new dominant marketing frameworks strategies, models, and analyses to acquire prospects and customers over time, help you set business goals and defined your purpose in business, and help with business awareness and business retention.

Should you want to use our strategical dominant frameworks marketing models; you will find how to use them in this playbook, our new competitor model analysis you will find how to use it and there is a practical example in this playbook, we encourage in this playbook to use our concept of a service catalogue for online distributions and our idea can be adapted to products, see how in this playbook, and download our service catalogue.

Girlfridayz 4 Sales Drivers ®
Audience Attraction complimentary Drivers Matrix

TM - Target Market
Who's your audience and how do you relate to your audience.

G - Guarantee
A promise with certainty that you will do what you prescribe.

IO - Irresistible Offer
A tempting offer to attract prospects.

CTA - Call to action
Short powerful text for prospects to act on content.

SP - Social Proof
Review by customers or prospects

Written by Trisha Amable — Girlfridayz — Website: https://girlfridayz.com
Girllfridayz number 10358020 girlfriday, girlfridayz^{tm} is a registered trademark in the UK

Figure 2 Girlfridayz Leads and Sales strategic Matrix

Using our playbook discover resources to help make your days more productive while you stay focused and connected to what is important for your business growth and increase profitability over time. How can this playbook and The Cellar help manage your well-being, reduce stress, and keep you on track throughout the year? It Is by following, and implementing the methodology and tactics including the strategies in this book and The Cellar.

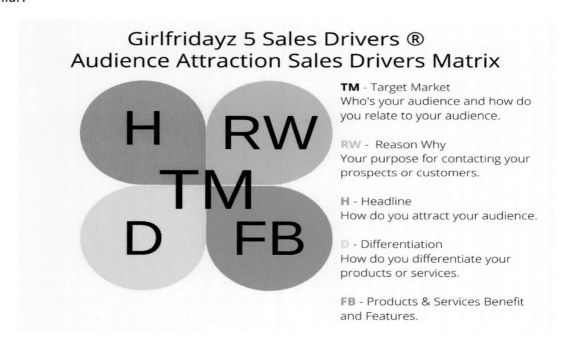

Written by Trisha Amable – Girlfridayz – Website: https://girlfridayz.com
Girllfridayz number 10358020 girlfriday, girlfridayz™ is a registered trademark in the UK

Playbook and System for winning

How to engineer growth in your small business

Tasks

Challenges

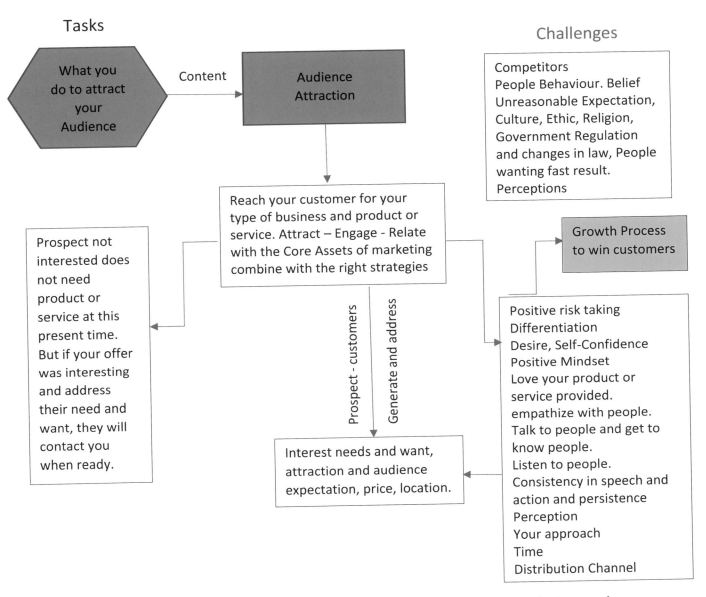

What you do to attract your Audience

Content →

Audience Attraction

Competitors
People Behaviour. Belief
Unreasonable Expectation,
Culture, Ethic, Religion,
Government Regulation
and changes in law, People
wanting fast result.
Perceptions

Reach your customer for your type of business and product or service. Attract – Engage - Relate with the Core Assets of marketing combine with the right strategies

Growth Process to win customers

Prospect not interested does not need product or service at this present time. But if your offer was interesting and address their need and want, they will contact you when ready.

Prospect - customers

Generate and address

Positive risk taking
Differentiation
Desire, Self-Confidence
Positive Mindset
Love your product or
service provided.
empathize with people.
Talk to people and get to
know people.
Listen to people.
Consistency in speech and
action and persistence
Perception
Your approach
Time
Distribution Channel

Interest needs and want, attraction and audience expectation, price, location.

Make sure your products or services make people see the value of having your product or service in their lives and include inspirational pictures that help with buying decisions.

Written by Trisha Amable – Girlfridayz – Website: https://girlfridayz.com
Girllfridayz number 10358020 girlfriday, girlfridayz^{tm} is a registered trademark in the UK

The Formula

Before I revealed the Core Assets, which is considered a formula as marketing is a science. It requires certain characteristics in the business using them. The characteristic needed is consistency in action, discipline, persistence, and a strong belief that they work. If you do not believe in the Core Assets' power, you will not use them daily to your advantage and will not make the necessary effort required to succeed.

When you believe that the Core Assets work you open your mind and have a positive attitude toward them, therefore you see the possibility of growing your business effortlessly and effectively. Having said that they are not magical you need to put the work in and, an effort to see the power of using the Core Assets with the right technique which is discussed in this playbook.

By now you must be dying to know what tactics I am referring to, hence without further ado here is the **formula $(TxLxCxM)^3$ S = exponential growth**.

Below are the 9 marketing tactics, and there are only 9 tactics. I have placed the tactics, and the Core Assets in a table for you to see at glance and will explain the formula component later.

The Core Assets of marketing

1. Target Market (TM)	
2. Headline (H)	6. Irresistible offer (IO)
3. Reason Why (RW)	7. Guarantee (G)
4. Differentiator (D)	8. Social Proof (SP)
5. Feature & Benefit (FB)	9. Call to Action (CTA)

The Periodic Table above depicts the Core Assets elements of marketing and they are part of a system when used together with strategies they amalgamate and become one this is called strategic marketing. It is like turning on the light switch if you think about it this way when

11

you press the light switch the current goes through the circuit and the light is on. The same process is used by the Core Assets, the magic of it is in the multiplying effect. I am going to explain each component of the formula now.

Transforming your existing sales

T: Transforming your existing sales and marketing refer to the 9 core elements, the tactics and each marketing piece when used with strategies and the correct technique for your sales and marketing works.

To experience massive success and grow your business exponentially in a relatively short period you need to use all the tactics together (**Target Market, Headline, Reason Why, differentiator, feature & benefit, Irresistible offer, guarantee, social proof, call to action**) because if you do not your result might not be as good as you hope, and your business will grow slowly.

The combination formula nCr = n! / r! * (n-r)! where n represents the total number of elements and r represents the number of elements being chosen at a time. Combinations are a way to calculate the total outcome of an event where the order of the outcome does not matter.

I am going to demonstrate in this example below how you could use the combination formula to help you use as many tactics as you can in your sales and marketing as well as what would be the best combination depending on the type of promotional marketing material used.

There is a total of 9 tactics hence n=9 then r= the number of tactics used, I am going to use only 6 tactics and I placed my numbers in the formula.

nCr = 9! / 6! *(9-6)!
$\qquad$ 9!/6! *3!
$\qquad$ 9!/18!
The result = 0.5! meaning you are not using three tactics.

If we translate this result into a percentage, you are using 95% of the Core Assets and leaving out 5%. It does not matter in which order you use the six tactics in your promotional marketing, however, using 6 Core Assets will produce a good outcome.

To get the best result using only 6 tactics you need to use TM, H, RW, FB, IO, and CTA this combination will increase your sales.

The beauty of the Core Assets of marketing is they are permuting too, and we can get a different number of permutations of the Core Assets of marketing where the tactics can be repeated for maximum effect and hook the customer.

The formulas for permutation are P(n,r) = n!/(n-r)! and for several different permutations, the formula is n!/n_1! N_2!...n_k! where n represents the total number of elements and r represents the number of elements being chosen at a time.

Written by Trisha Amable – Girlfridayz – Website: https://girlfridayz.com
Girllfridayz number 10358020 girlfriday, girlfridayz[tm] is a registered trademark in the UK

Permutation is a way to calculate the total outcome of an event where the order of the outcome does matter. Using my earlier example of 6 tactics, here is how the 9 Core Assets of marketing permute.

$P(9,6) = 9!/(9-6)$

$P(9,6) = 3!$

The result 3! Mean the tactics are permuting because you can use 6 of the 9 tactics where the order matters. Meaning you can use TM, H, RW, FB, CTA, and D from my example of using 6 tactics. The tactics permute in that order TM, H, RW, FB, CTA the D is mainly part of the combination as you could have used a G instead of D or an IO instead of a D and SP instead of D.

Still using the example here, the number of different permutations of the tactics where the tactics are repeated items.

$9! / 9_1! \, 9_2! \, 9_3! \, 9_4! \, 9_5! \, 9_6! = 54/9$

The result is 6 tactics used.

The result means that you can use 6 different permutations tactics repeating the same tactics in your marketing messages like TM, H, RW, RW, FB, and CTA.

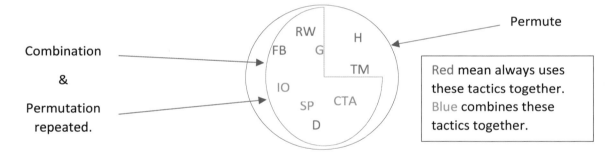

The picture below demonstrates two businesses in different industries using only a few tactics in their flyers they can achieve sales but not major sales as one business is only using three tactics and the other using two only.

Affordable Tree Care picture below does not use any headline and their business name could be confused with a headline, they are using a differentiator as they mentioned that they specialized in fruit trees, and their flyers have social proof displayed because NPTC and City & Guild and two offers free quote and free advice.

On the other hand, Gitas Portal has a headline "your personal store invitation a 10% offer with the flyer" and a CTA saying Delicious Curvy Range Now Available.

Written by Trisha Amable – Girlfridayz – Website: https://girlfridayz.com
Girllfridayz number 10358020 girlfriday, girlfridayz[tm] is a registered trademark in the UK

Confusing headline

Offer

Social Proof

Differentiator

CTA

Deliciously Curvy range
NOW AVAILABLE

offer

10% OFF
with this flyer

headline

One flyer does not have any strategy behind it and the tactic are in used and too much information this kind of flyers will attract customers but would not get them huge revenue or increase profit either. Both companies did not mention the reason why we should use them nor the feature or benefit they offer and no guarantee either.

Flyers two uses more tactics and demonstrates their differentiator via picture as they specialised in African clothing and informed people via picture and a CTA text that curvy people can buy from their store as they are now inclusive and aimed at women only.

We changed the flyer's contents of one business to demonstrate to you that we have used 6 tactics in their flyer to maximise lead and sales.

1) Affordable Tree Care

How you too can have a beautiful garden (h)

We are a family run business with 15yrs experience pruning trees and shrubs under our belt and we specialised in Fruit Trees. (D) We have a host of services available to ensure that your trees, hedges, and shrubs remain in a perfect condition and are the envy of your neighbour and we are now working in your area. (RW)

You benefit of our expertise in tree care, and you can trust us to deliver an excellent service to you at an affordable price that you can trust. (B)

In need of tree care? call us today to get free advice for your tree and a free quote (CTA & IO)

Tel: 0208 485 8621 M: 07920 026 769 (SP)   NPTC Registered   City & Guild

---

Lead Generation

L: Lead generation refers to the process of generating leads gaining potential customers interested in what you have to offer or creating interest in what you have to offer. In lead generation, each strategy needs the core element therefore you need to use the Core Assets with your lead generation strategy it is like betting on a sure thing.

Therefore, a headline is particularly important as most people will read the title if the title does not interest them chances are the rest of the content is binned or ignored. Whatever promotional material or method you use your headline greatly matter.

Reaching your customers in a deeply emotional way is a key to successful copywriting and research has shown that headline is the unquestionable most important piece of copy used to reach prospects and obtain conversion. The following table below from the Advance Marketing Institution demonstrates the importance of using powerful words in three classifications to attract leads and conversion.

Intellectual	Empathetic	Spiritual
Words which are especially effective when offering products and services that require reasoning or careful evaluation.	Words which resonate in with Empathetic impact often bring out profound and strong positive emotional reactions in people.	Words which have the strongest potential for influence and often appeal to people at a very deep emotional level.

1. picture source from the Advance Marketing Institution

Your headline should use words with intellectual conation as they are especially effective when offering products or services that require reasoning or careful evaluation.

Intellectual impact words are best used to attune copy and sales messages aimed at people and businesses involved in the fields of education, law, medicine, research, politics, and similar fields. While not restricted to these groups, by giving presentations which are weighted with Intellectual impact words, your clients and customers will be a more positive influence and you are more likely to attain a more favourable response.

Your headline should use words with empathetic conation as they bring out profound and strong positive emotional reactions in people **Such Oil of Olay keeps the doctors at bay** both intellectual and emphatic.

However, using more words with Empathetic impact delivers desirable conversion responses from those types of market segments caregiving. For example, nurses, doctors, and counsellors all tend to respond easily and favourably to Empathetic words. Women, and especially mothers, are very strong in their use of Empathetic impact words in the language.

While the use of Empathetic impact words does not have to be limited to these groups, we have found that selecting more words with Empathetic impact delivers desirable conversion responses from those types of market segments.

Your headline should use words with spiritual conation which have the strongest potential for influencing people and often appeal to people at a very deep emotional level.

Words that resonate with Spiritual impact are the smallest number of words in the language. AMI research has found that Spiritual impact words carry the strongest potential for influence and often appeal to people at a very deep emotional level. Like **Eat five fruits per day and feel like a new you**

Words with Spiritual impact are best used with people and businesses desiring to appeal to some aspect of spirituality. This does not mean religion specifically, but any product or service that resonates with "spirituality" oriented markets are appropriate.

The clergy, new age, health food and related markets all respond favourably to sales copy heavy with Spiritual impact content. Women and children also respond strongly to words in the Spiritual sphere. Marketing documents with strong Spiritual impact content can make for the most powerful presentations in the marketplace but must be used with considerable skill.

As you can see headline is the most important component of the Core Assets here are 20 effective headlines templates that work

Here are 20 effective headlines to start you off by combining the different types of headlines with the proven headline templates below and you automatically create winning headlines combine them with power words in the three categories mention above and you have a winning combination. We've tested all the headlines in our templates, and they got the power to convert into sales as they are hitting the three categories (intellectual, empathetic, and spiritual) Emotional Marketing Value. However neutral headline is less popular but does attract people therefore negative keywork do work too and should be part of your marketing arsenal. Have you ever heard of the saying the most boring think are the most important ones and you usually get the most result? We've had a few with no score or emotional marketing value it does not mean they are not successful headlines but just short.

20 Effective Headline Templates

Simply add the missing word to form a new headline of your own related to your business or one from the template and modify it to suit your need.

1. They did not think I could .... but I did.
   Ex: They laughed when I sat down at the piano but when I started to play, they fell silent in amazement. (scored 15% EMV – intellectual, empathetic, and spiritual)

   Ex: They did not think I could be good at studying, but I prove them wrong by getting my degree (scored 26.32% EMV – intellectual)

Written by Trisha Amable – Girlfridayz – Website: https://girlfridayz.com
Girllfridayz number 10358020 girlfriday, girlfridayz^{tm} is a registered trademark in the UK

Ex: They did not think I could grow my business, but I did in less than three years (scored 11.76% EMV – intellectual & empathetic)

2. Who else wants.....?
Ex: Who wants an extra hour a day (scored 28.57% EMV – both spiritual and empathetic)

   Ex: Who wants more traffic to their website (Scored 42.86 EMV -spiritual)

   Ex: Who wants to lose 5kg to feel healthier (scored 87.5% EMV -spiritual)

3. How To ….Get, Have, Acquire, Solve, Profit, Own etc – the biggest benefit you got

   Ex: How to manage your computer (scored 33.33% EMV – spiritual)

   Ex: How to lose 10kg eating healthier food (scored 71.43% EMV - spiritual)

   Ex: How to solve this simple math equation (scored 28.7% EMV – empathetic and spiritual)

4. How….Made Me …

   Ex: How a "fool start" made me a star salesman (scored 44.44% EMV – empathetic)

   Ex: How this drink made me healthier (scored 33.33% - intellectual)

   Ex: How my mentor turned me into a successful entrepreneur (scored 33.33% EMV – intellectual, empathic and spiritual)

5. Are You….?

   Ex: Are you smarter than your brother (scored 50% EMV – empathetic)

   Ex: Are you ready to retire (scored 120% EMV – intellectual)

   Ex: Are you ready to stop smoking (scored 83.33% EMV – empathetic, spiritual)

6. For (type of person) How to

   Ex: For busy director: How to educate new patients in half the time (scored 41.67% - spiritual)

   Ex: For students: How to pass your exam without being overwhelmed (scored 30% - spiritual)

   Ex: For nervous people: How to beat nervousness (scored 42.86% - intellectual)

7. Have you….?

Written by Trisha Amable – Girlfridayz – Website: https://girlfridayz.com
Girllfridayz number 10358020 girlfriday, girlfridayz[tm] is a registered trademark in the UK

Ex: Have you ever thought of investing in property (scored 37.5% EMV – intellectual, empathetic, spiritual)

Ex: Have you got a mentor to help you grow your business (scored 36.36 EMV – spiritual)

EX: Have you made your million yet (scored 16.67% EMV – spiritual)

8. Have you heard…?

Ex: Have you heard of the latest development in technology (scored 33.33% EMV – intellectual, empathetic, spiritual)

Ex: Have you heard of the latest craze: drink cherry soda (scored 20% EMV intellectual, spiritual)

Ex: Have you heard of Alvoxcon A700 apparently, it's a must-have (scored 18.18% EMV -intellectual, spiritual)

9. When to… When….?

Ex: When is the best time to go to university (scored 44.44% EMV – spiritual)

Ex: When can you get married to your loved one legally (scored 40% EMV intellectual, Spiritual)

Ex: When is your birthday we have a surprise for you (scored 20% EMV – intellectual, spiritual)

10. Where to….where….?

Ex: Where is the best place to go in Essex (scored 11.11% EMV – spiritual)

Ex: Where can you find the best restaurant in London (scored 33.33% EMV – empathetic)

Ex: Here are 10 places where you can eat for a tenner (scored 27.27% EMV – spiritual)

11. What….?

Ex: What made me a millionaire (scored 20% EMV – intellectual)

Ex: Here is what can be done to improve your spelling (scored 33.33% EMV – spiritual)

Ex: What is before 3 and after 6 (scored 14.29% EMV – intellectual)

12. Do not miss out …..?

EX: Do not miss out on the Z56 our most advanced mobile phone (scored 33.33% EMV – empathetic)

Ex: Offer expired in 2 days – do not miss out on this fantastic offer (Scored 23.08% EMV – empathetic)

Written by Trisha Amable – Girlfridayz – Website: https://girlfridayz.com
Girllfridayz number 10358020 girlfriday, girlfridayz^{tm} is a registered trademark in the UK

Ex: Do not miss out our celebration cake sale and your chance to win a prize (scored 26.67% EMV – empathetic, spiritual)

13. It could be… could you be…?

    Ex: It could be you the winner of our fundraising race (scored 30% EMV - intellectual, empathetic, spiritual)

    Ex: Play lifewithmore#win you could be the winner of £100 (scored 30% EMV - intellectual, empathetic, spiritual)

    Ex: Could it be MJ copycat who I met on the train (scored 45.45% EMV - intellectual, empathetic)

14. Get…?

    Ex: Get your bikini body just in time for summer (scored 33.33% EMV - intellectual)

    Ex: Get fit in 6 weeks with this new G2T diet drink (scored 18.18% EMV – intellectual, spiritual)

    Ex: Get our latest Book titled The Raven Haven [bestseller] (scored 12.50% EMV – empathetic)

15. The importance of…. It's important to….

    Ex: The importance of a PESTEL Analysis (scored 0.00% EMV - Neutral)

    Ex: The Importance of a PEST Analysis (scored 0.00% EMV- Neutral)

    Ex: It's important to use titles to rank higher (scored 37.5% EMV - Spiritual)

16. You invited…Your personal invitation

    Ex: You're invited to our grand opening (scored 50% EMV - Spiritual)

    Ex: Your personal invitation to our monthly meeting (scored 57.14% EMV - intellectual)

    Ex: You are invited to our celebration lunch (scored 50% EMV - spiritual)

17. Exclusive… (take an exclusive, Get exclusive, the most exclusive…)

    Ex: Exclusive content do not miss it (scored 66.67 EMV - empathetic, spiritual)

    Ex: Get exclusive access to our marketing Bootcamp (scored 57.14% EMV- empathetic, spiritual)

    Ex: [Exclusive] the most beautiful sightseen you have ever seen (scored 37.5% EMV - spiritual)

18. Secret….

    Ex: Secret reveal (could not get a score on this one)

Written by Trisha Amable – Girlfridayz – Website: https://girlfridayz.com
Girllfridayz number 10358020 girlfriday, girlfridayz[tm] is a registered trademark in the UK

Ex: The hidden secret of the diamond mine reveal (scored 25% EMV - intellectual)

Ex: The most guarded secret gets the first peek (scored 37.50 EMV– intellectual)

19. Tip or tips....

Ex: 10 business tips to grow your business (scored 14.29 – spiritual)

Ex: Looking for business tips? If you, do you come to the right place (scored 30.77% EMV – spiritual)

Ex: Cooking tips to spice up your meal (scored 28.57 EMV – intellectual, spiritual)

20. Hack...

Ex: The best technique to hack success (scored 33.33% EMV – intellectual, spiritual)

Ex: 10 growth hacks (no score on that one)

Ex: It is a marketing hack (scored 25% EMV – Empathetic)

To understand the Emotional Marketing Value percentage in this headline template you need to know what is counted. The percentage indicates the number of EMV words used to form the sentence and then the words are compared with the criterion in the categories after selecting an industry and then the result of the comparison is given in percentage.

The score that my headline template scored is above average and I have one score over 100% and eight scored under 20% but all headlines belong to a category, therefore, contained words with emotional marketing value and help achieve conversion.

For you to understand the English language contains 20% of EMV words. It is said that most professional copywriters' headlines will have **30%-40% EMV words in their headlines**, while the most gifted copywriters will have **50%-75% EMV words in their headlines**. A perfect score would be 100%, but that is rare unless your headline is less than five words.

Therefore, you can use these headlines to help you start up as they are proven to work and you will acquire leads. If you use all the Core Assets in your marketing, you will acquire leads it's just as easy with all the tactics and strategies social proof and testimonials to acquire prospects without spending a huge amount on your advertising.

How to get testimonials fast

It can be difficult to acquire testimonials because most customers when you asked them, would say yes; I do it but do not or I have difficulties giving you an online testimonial or leave their comment on your social media and you do not always have the time to cut and paste the comment and paste it on your testimonial page of your website.

There is a fast way to ensure testimonials by posting a letter to your existing customers including a self-stamp envelope with your return address. People will fill the back of your letter and return it to you for free and there you have it a collection of social proof.

Written by Trisha Amable – Girlfridayz – Website: https://girlfridayz.com
Girllfridayz number 10358020 girlfriday, girlfridayz^tm is a registered trademark in the UK

The template can be customised with your details of your products or services you would like a review, and you will need to add the name of each customer. If you have a lot of customers, you want a review using the mail merge function in Microsoft Word. It helps you put all addresses quickly instead of writing them one by one.

This work is a treat and people do tend to send your letter back to you with their testimonial at the back due to the incentive inserted in the envelope a return reply envelope already stamped. Therefore, no cost to the client and they feel more inclined to give you a testimonial as all they need to do is to post it back to you.

You may feel that you are paying for a comment, but social proof is gold dust, and a section of people based their decision to purchase your product or service on your review alone on occasions regardless if you have an offer or guarantee in place for their decision will rest on the review comment. Hence, it is important to have a few social proofs to show when require as they can increase profitability. Have you heard of the saying "give a little and you shall receive"?

Customer testimonials are the diamond of your business and without them, you do not have a business therefore what a customer says about your business is gold dust so to speak and their testimonial is essential for growth.

Whether be a positive comment or a negative customer comment these comments help you improve in many ways your sales because they buy from you, it's good for your business because if you get a good comment, you do not rest on it you try to improve your product or service or customer service to remain on top because complacency can kill your business over time. If you get a negative review, it is an opportunity for you to see the area you can change and improve based on the comment made.

Therefore, customer testimonials are an important part of your business growth. They can help immensely with your conversion rate of visitors to your business and an increase in profit can be seen in months. Testimonials add weight to your use of your Assets, and they are easy to get especially if the customers feel appreciated and not pressured to give any comments. Genuine reviews are worth gold, you might be tempted to put your own reviews, but customers can see them miles away as they do not appear genuine, and you will not get a good result and it will affect your sale negatively.

Many people do not realise how hard it can be to persuade someone to open their wallet for the first time on an unknown website or to buy from an unknown trade person. Therefore, Testimonials can be the push the buyer need to be convinced.

Testimonial by the dozen letter Sale Accelerator template letter

Name & Address

Good Morning [Name of customer]

I have a favour to ask you.

21

Written by Trisha Amable – Girlfridayz – Website: https://girlfridayz.com
Girllfridayz number 10358020 girlfriday, girlfridayz^{tm} is a registered trademark in the UK

I am in the process of putting together a list of testimonials – a collection of comments about my ABC Product Service from satisfied clients/customers/patients like yourself.

Would you take a few minutes of your time to give me your opinion of my ABC Product Service? No need to dictate a letter just jot your comment on the back of this letter and return it in the envelope provided.

I look forward to learning what you like about my ABC Product Service and I also welcome any suggestions or criticism. many thanks

Kind Regards

Your Name

Title

You have my permission to quote from the attached letter in ads, brochures, direct mail, PR, and other marketing materials to promote your service (add signature & Date)

Online Adaptation of the template Testimonial by the Dozen letter

The template Testimonial by the Dozen sales accelerator can be adapted online to your network if you build a following and people like your content posted or participate in the community and engage with other people's posts. You can try this version which we try with our connection and public on LinkedIn.

We could do this because we have over 18k connections and the public even 1st-degree connections asked us for connections people are aware of our brand Girlfridayz, and we have achieved good momentum on this platform. Here below is the post with the adapted template for social media.

We wrote a Letter using Microsoft word and PDF it so we could upload it on LinkedIn using the upload document function.

Good Morning my LinkedIn Family (H)(inbound strategy) Posted 1 week ago

I have a favour to ask you, I am in the process of putting together a list of testimonials – a collection of comments about my engagement with you on LinkedIn from satisfied posts replied by myself or support provided to you free of charge from direct messages and you were happy with the support given. (RW)

Would you take a few minutes of your time to give me your opinion on the above? (CTA) No need to dedicate a full post just your comment in the comments or direct message me.

I look forward to learning what you like about my support through engagement, and I also welcome any suggestions or criticism many thanks for taking part.

Written by Trisha Amable – Girlfridayz – Website: https://girlfridayz.com
Girllfridayz number 10358020 girlfriday, girlfridayz tm is a registered trademark in the UK

Kind regards

Trisha Patricia Amable
CEO of Girlfridayz Limited

I also conducted market testing to gather which group would respond favourably.

Connection 61 views 2 likes and one comment DNB "Trisha, your consistency and your insight are amazing and great, keep up the good work and don't stop."

Public 96 views no likes and no comments.

When you do A/B testing – market testing it is good to leave it for at least three to 6 months to gather better metrics and decide on the result. My post was done a week ago the 13/07/20 and I wrote this result feedback on 20/07/20.

The Perfect Prospect List

Most businesses are successful but are bad at getting prospects because they do not use all methods available at their reach. Did you know that businesses who are already spending on marketing are your perfect prospect if you are a business consultant because they are seeking strategies and tactics to grow their business therefore you can contact them and offer your service or product?

The perfect Prospect List:

- Businesses spending money on Marketing & Advertising
- Local Newspaper ads
- Local Magazine ads
- Business Directories listing
- Direct Mail
- Flyers receive through your door.
- Google Ads, Facebook, Yell.com, LinkedIn
- Business Card
- Forum website wanted categories.
- Attending local Event
- Speaking at event
- Word of Mouth
- Speaking about your business
- Amazon Alexa
- Amazon review
- Joining group
- Sale letter
- Special report
- Free website reviews

- Factsheet
- Gumtree classified ads.
- Supermarket hall where you can put your banner and product on display.
- Bark.com

Apart from email marketing, most businesses do not do the above or seldomly do the above to access people and convert them into leads which can turn into paying customers. All these sources above have a great potential to churn out leads by the dozen should you make the effort to look carefully at every one of these free tools to get potential customers using your business.

The same way you received through your door an interesting flyer you would them contact the person for more information or use their service or purchase the product well the same goes for you if you see an ad, where someone is requesting your services or product contact them and speak to them about your product or services. When you attend an event, it is not because you do not have a stand or cubicle that you cannot access potential leads. You can approach them and speak about your business to them and what you can do for their business.

We get leads by conducting free website reviews for website owners and it works we do get customers through doing this or participating in the conversation on LinkedIn by posting interesting posts and replying to comments. We increased our connection and got a few leads and converted them into paying customers.

Remember every lead generation strategy needs the core elements the Core Assets without them your strategy will not be effective. Whether you are pitching your business to a potential client using your voice you need to include about three tactics.

How I acquire our new customers using the Core Assets

I met this prospect in my local area last year we started chatting and he told me he runs a property business and cleaning service, I told him I am marketing and I support businesses with marketing to start up or grow their business, website design and more. I asked if he had a website, and he replied he does, and I offer to review his website for free. (Lead magnet) He agreed and give us his website address.

We completed a Detailed Review for him on 5th July 2018 with recommendations and told him we could fix all issues identified and add information about us and our website design price.

He never replied to my email but this year 21st June 2019 I received a call it was him telling me do you remember you did a free website review for me last year? I replied yes, I do and asked for his name and email address. He gave me his details over the phone and I went to my email and found the review completed for him and said did you fix the issues.

Written by Trisha Amable – Girlfridayz – Website: https://girlfridayz.com
Girllfridayz number 10358020 girlfriday, girlfridayz^{tm} is a registered trademark in the UK

He replied no, my previous developer is no longer working, and I do not know how to fix the issues that is why I am calling you as you are a website designer, and you did my website review last year and it is very good he added can I have an appointment tomorrow.

I replied yes that's fine can you come at 1 pm he replied perfect.

How I used the Core Assets in my speech to get a new customer using a tripwire and gentle persuasion.

I was prepared for our meeting I put his website on my TV screen so he could see it and I noticed that no change had been made.

He attended and I demonstrated to him all the areas which needed to be fixed on his website and he informed me that he understood. He added that he noticed duplicated pages I replied yes plus other issues, and I guess you not getting many visitors.

He replied barely any. I replied it is because your services are not on the front page, the text is barely visible, too many unnecessary animations and wrong information written and added your website is a customer's turn off and you cannot achieve a sale through it let alone get leads.

I added we can fix this easy for you and your visitor count will increase, we can give it a modern look as it looks dated and has good navigation, put your service in front view and improve your content. I then say to him let me show you a superbly designed website he replied yes.

I had our website opened on another tab already. I clicked on the tab and my website loaded and I asked him to view it. He clicked on my entry point to get started and he view my homepage with my services. I asked him what you see, he replied, my services. I told him to go to your site and what do you see on your homepage he replied, information about me.

I replied your about page should not be the first thing people see but what you offer should be on display your cleaning services and property service. Your (about page) should be on another page.

I told him to continue viewing my website and added clicked what interest you, he clicked on the online presence link and went to our website design page.

I discussed our website bundle package offers and informed him of the package best suited for his website revamp should he decide to use us. He replied he is interested in the business package, and I replied; that the business package is the right choice for you and you get all this for only £710 we can revamp your website using your existing content. He replied he will need an updated text and possibly a new picture and he has a logo already. I replied we can add your existing logo.

He thought for a minute and said that £710 is too much I am a small business, and I am pressed for funds at present. I replied we offer a payment facility for payments over £200 and you will need to request it.

Written by Trisha Amable – Girlfridayz – Website: https://girlfridayz.com
Girllfridayz number 10358020 girlfriday, girlfridayz^{tm} is a registered trademark in the UK

I added we can do this for you as a goodwill gesture we offer you 20% discount on the original price and I calculated the discounted price and told him £568 is £142 off and the discount offer expired in 24 hours (the irresistible offer) and added If you decide to use us you need to decide today, (CTA) and you will benefit of 20% discount, therefore, the price offer is £568 today (Benefit and CTA).

He replied I want to use you to design my website for me, but I can only afford £500. I replied no I cannot it is £568 or £710 your choice the discount expired tomorrow (Tripwire) and said £568, and we send your order confirmation today and the deposit required would be £284 payable within a month of the order date. (Gentle Persuasion)

He thought about what I said and said ok you offer me a discount which expires in 24 hours on Sunday. I replied yes that's right it expires in 24hrs therefore on Sunday and it is £568 for your business website and added could I please have your email address? (**See Analysis of my customer acquisition**)

He replied you got it already and I am looking forward to starting to work with you. I replied I am looking forward to working with you too, do you need us to do your text for you, (cross-sell) He replied yes you do it. I replied we charge £395 for website copywriting. He replied no, I cannot afford it I will provide you with a text and I replied that fine thank you. (Customer agreement)

The meeting terminated and I captured his details and said thank you for your order. He replied thank you and added a very good meeting. (On-the-spot feedback from customers).

I replied, thanks and I will send you our documents and a client design brief, please complete them fully as we need to design your website according to your need. He replied oh, do I need to it is a bit difficult for me to look at the text on my website.

I replied if you have any difficulties completing our form, we can support you to complete them and added you will need to book an appointment for this service. He replied I will. (Good customer service)

Analysis of my customer acquisition

The example above demonstrates to you how I secure a new customer. You can see that my lead magnet worked I completed a free website review for the prospective leads and nearly a year later he contacted me about the review completed and requested an appointment.

This shows that if you do a free review, a special report, factsheet, a guide any other type of publication as a **lead magnet** the content must be excellent and valuable for the potential customers as they will contact you when they need you and remember what you have done for them for free.

When you send a **lead magnet** ensure that you capture the details of your potential prospect because later you can send a pertaining offer which might be interesting to the prospect and

Written by Trisha Amable – Girlfridayz – Website: https://girlfridayz.com
Girllfridayz number 10358020 girlfriday, girlfridayz^{tm} is a registered trademark in the UK

they might contact you for further information, arrange an appointment or purchase your offer straight away.

We also used marketing strategies I first demonstrated all the errors on his website and explained how they can be corrected therefore demonstrating my expertise in website design and I asked if he wanted to see a good design website. I directed him to my website, and I sold him my services without selling them. I did this by telling him to tell me what he sees still part of our conversation which he replied, my services.

I then went to his website and asked what he sees on his website and he replied to my about page. I explained further about the placement of an about page on a website and then asked to go back to my site and look for our about page.

He looked and said I cannot see it I showed him where it is, and it is on my homepage accessible by a link. I then said what services interested you, he clicked on website design and viewed our website bundle packages. I told him the various website type available and added the best one for you is the business website package and you get all this for only £710.

He thought about it and then said he was a small business and pressed for cash. I first informed him of our payment facility for payment over £200 then offer him a discount of 20% which expire in 24hrs and calculated the price of the package and said £568 you benefit of £184 off.

After thinking about it he tried to get a bargain and lower the price by then I knew he wanted to use our service I said no and offer a tripwire by saying £568 or £710 and offer the choice by saying it your choice and added £568 and we will send you your confirmation of order today which is a call to action.

After a pause he said you did not need to do all this I was going to use your service to design my website anyway. I replied £710 then. He replied you offer me a discount which expires in 24hrs on Sunday. I replied 20% the offer expired in 24hrs do you want to take the offer? He replied yes £568. I replied I send you your confirmation of order today.

Do you see how I sold my services without selling and won over the prospect who is now my customer? I even offer further support part of customer care by stating I can complete with him our documents, but he needs to arrange an appointment and he said yes.

My new customer was so pleased with his first meeting with me that he gave me on-the-spot feedback by saying a particularly good meeting.

You see how it is easy to use the Core Assets and strategies together to achieve positive results and a sale. It works like magic just like the example above you need to use the strategies and Core Assets in your sales pitch, your written content, social media post, sales letter, and contacting prospect on the phone because they do work and discipline and persistence helps but if it fails it not tar you just need to try something else and if you find a strategy and tactics who works systemised it and use it when needed over and over again this way you will increase your sales and profit.

Written by Trisha Amable – Girlfridayz – Website: https://girlfridayz.com
Girllfridayz number 10358020 girlfriday, girlfridayz[tm] is a registered trademark in the UK

What not to do when selling your service to persuade a prospective client

I have promoted heavily this very book that you are reading now on LinkedIn and generated lots of interest, got a few connections requests and several positive replies and achieved sales 4 other eBooks (cross-sell) by informing the prospect to purchase a business plan template and guide when discussing his website proposal via Skype and the prospect became my client for his social website design in the process just by using the Core Assets of marketing in my message and persistence with definiteness of purpose in mind and decision as I am determined to sell 20 copies for starters to the wealthiest mastermind mind brain who believe in the power of the Core Assets of marketing.

Before I delve into a conversation with one of my connections on LinkedIn that I identified as a possible prospect to purchase this playbook after replying to niceties. Let me show you the inbound marketing strategy combining the Core Assets to achieve the latter positive results.

I bet you are curious and want to know what was said to get such a positive result in such a short time by now here it is:

Person Name Think and Grow Rich (headline)with The Core Assets of Marketing Playbook and The Core Assets of Marketing Startup Kit Playbook - Purchase the Playbook today(call to action) Person Name if you want to grow your existing business or start-up business as the time is now 2020 is the time to start and do not be fazed by the price which is minimal compared to the valuable, useful specialized knowledge you will gain using the Playbook and up your revenue 20 times fold within a year of using it (RW and benefit). https://lnkd.in/dQYSPcM Click on the link and GET IT TODAY Got it (CTA)

You can see that my message uses inbound strategies with the personalisation calling the prospect by his or her name then I tucked in the headline and attached it to the product followed by an inline call to action a definite demand soften by mentioning the prospect's name again. Swiftly followed by the reason why I want the prospect to purchase this playbook and highlighting the benefit they will gain purchasing it. Tuck in the link showing where to purchase it and finish with a strong call to action and confirmation of understanding.

Further to my increased connection on LinkedIn, I found myself conversing with another possible prospect who initiated the chat, and he was a pushy salesman, to say the least here is what not to do when selling your service to persuade a prospect client below when selling your services.

Recall the conversation below carefully read J and my replies, you may notice what not to do yourself if you feel inclined to do so to achieve a sale at all costs. Maybe he was on the quota and pressured to achieve sales at all costs by wearing out the prospect to submission, this strategy might work on some people but is not recommended.

He started by asking me where I was from, I replied, France but lives in London UK. Then how are you doing? I replied I am doing fine, He replied that is good to hear. I asked where he was from, and he replied, Germany, I replied that's great, he replied welcome what do you do?

Written by Trisha Amable – Girlfridayz – Website: https://girlfridayz.com
Girllfridayz number 10358020 girlfriday, girlfridayz™ is a registered trademark in the UK

When I saw this question, I thought let me use my message above to inform him what I do and mentioned this playbook.

Here is what I say: Marketing I run my own business https://girlfridayz.com J would you be interested in Think and Grow Rich with The Core Assets of Marketing Playbook and The Core Assets of Marketing Start-up Kit Playbook - Purchase the Playbook today J if you want to grow your existing business or start-up business as the time is now 2020 is the time to start and do not be fazed by the price which is minimal compared to the valuable, useful specialized knowledge you will gain using the Playbook and up your revenue 20 times fold within a year of using it. https://lnkd.in/dQYSPcM Click on the link and GET IT TODAY Got it.

And I added I also write business and marketing publications.

He replies with a thumb emoji up to show his appreciation followed by are you open to online opportunities, that can earn you a consistent side income weekly? I reply yes what are you proposing? He replied have you heard of Bitcoin mining investment, then are you with me before I could reply. I replied yes, I tried it before.

J replied Good, is a nice lucrative business then followed by an explanation of what is Bitcoin "Bitcoin is a cryptocurrency and is a financial option in which when you trade with a small amount you receive a higher amount." He added that he usually tells people that there is nothing like free money or free bitcoins, you must mine for it, you must earn it.

My reply: it can depend on the invested amount, and I know all about Bitcoin. He replied I would like you to invest in our company with a minimum of $500 you can earn up to $4000 in a week of trade.

I replied not now, but do you have any information such as leaflets about your company or a website to view?

He replied, sure hit me up via What's App, I replied ok what's your website and view my website you get my number, and I sent you two links.

He replied with his number and say What's App number welcome I expect your text. I replied, your company website please, J replied with the link to the company he works for.

I found him on what's app and J continue pushing the Bitcoin in my face to try to convince me to sign up and create an account as well as invest. If you follow our direct message conversation I already said no, I was not interested at present but want more information about the company on LinkedIn.

I message him on what's app Hi J, what is your company name and website, he replied with the website link and just click on it, replied ok, thanks, he replied, his working under the company, I replied I guess so, he added Am just the Senior Account Manager okay. I replied I am working for my own company; I am the CEO of Girlfridayz Limited. He replied that's nice. I gave J the link to my website.

Written by Trisha Amable – Girlfridayz – Website: https://girlfridayz.com
Girllfridayz number 10358020 girlfriday, girlfridayz^tm is a registered trademark in the UK

I did not offer for him to view my website I sensed that J was disinterested in my business but only interested in selling me his services. I deducted this by his reply to our DM on LinkedIn and what's app message see how I was right below.

J replied I believe you will enjoy trading with our company ignoring my website link, I replied need more info, and I believe that your company would be a perfect candidate for our marketing playbook The Core Assets of Marketing to learn how to market your Bitcoin to the right crowd.

J replied "We have sophisticated trading technology and software which give us good strategies and signals to make sure your profits are guaranteed. Well, I have been with Forex/cryptocurrency trader and miner with 5 years of experience in the stock market.

I have been an expert trader for more than 3 years now and I got over 233 clients I have traded for. I have been able to yield a good number of profits daily and weekly to all my investors. What is required of you is you set up a live portfolio trading account on our website after that you'll make an investment deposit to your live portfolio trading account.

I'll be the one to take care of all trading activities on your behalf. You're allowed to monitor your trading account 24/7 a week. Our investment plans are affordable/available to all classes of investors be you a low earner or a millionaire, you're both welcomed and treated equally. Feel free to ask questions regarding/related to our services.

You notice his long reply after I said I need more information and that his company would be a good fit for this playbook. He ignore my replied and provided his credential, the trading platform, and instructed me on what to do and that it be responsible for my account.

I replied, click on the link I sent you on LinkedIn. J replied Are you interested in trading with our company? I replied I did all this before with another company and they steal my money bad experience twice shy.

J replied you are in a safe hand; all you need to do is register with the company website. You have access to monitor your live trading account as I trade for you. I can help you to trade and manage your profits daily that's if you are interested. Your trade account will be monitored by you to ensure everything is going on properly, your account can be monitored with your phone and computer device you choose to use.

I replied I viewed your website I will certainly think of trying in six months but not now J.

J replied you are not serious, have a nice day. I replied I am serious and entitled to think thoroughly about it.

J replied Bitcoin is very high now, and this is the right time to invest and earn a good profit, we are Licence and trusted. He uploaded two certificate pictures for me to view.

I got annoyed slightly at being ignored and I am the prospect in this case. I replied so you said, and I will look into it in six months, you are not in my purse, or you are not running my company for me, therefore you cannot tell me when to access your company J pushy salesman and sales technic never works, you need to listen to your prospective client.

I added I told you that you are a good candidate for my Playbook, The Core Assets of Marketing revealed purchased it today and with the money paid I may invest sooner than predicted and put the link of the playbook on my online store.

He realised what I said and replied Anytime you are ready. followed by a video testimonial of some guy who used their service alright can I see your picture? I replied by uploading my video of my playbook and commenting purchase it anytime you need it to improve your existing marketing strategy and tactic you are Bitcoin, and my expertise is marketing and I thoroughly think that you need it J.

He replies can you send me a picture. I replied, it's on the playbook cover, he replied send it to me "oga" bye. I replied play the video and I am more serious than you but instead, he send me his picture. J added send me your picture you are more than I d.o.t

I uploaded my picture which is on the paybook and said Trisha's owner of Girlfridayz, He replied I have seen this on your profile (LinkedIn Profile), and I need a new one. I replied, why J replied just send it ok I want to know you more. I took a selfie and send it. J replied Wow that's nice are you married? I replied just watch my video you see the same person talking and that's too much question, J replied lol I replied, personal questions I do not do. J replied sorry about that okay bye for now since you don't want to talk to me.

I purposely draw the conversation back in by saying this is a very recent pic of me I just took a selfie and added you look like my friend Leo. He sends me another picture of him in reply and a Really. I replied yes, I just watched your video about some guy testimonials about your company, J replied yeah, I replied Now watch my video about my playbook that is nice it is called reciprocal marketing.

J replied I be glad to do business with you, I replied Maybe but if you want to do business with my company you need to pay interest in it. J looked at the playbook message and replied that was nice of you followed by Join my company and two more quotes' pictures ("you must spend money to make money Plutus" and "Earn $32,500 within 7 days with your invested capital of $5,000".

I replied here is my catalogue of services, so you know what service we provide and give him the link. J replied I must confess you are beautiful. I replied thank you for the compliment and I have told you six months I meant it. J replied welcome have a nice day. I replied thank you click on my catalogue good night. J replied, good night.

In summary, the pushy salesman sees he started with a good opening and then did not wait for my replied that set me off and I knew that he was going to try to convince me to sign up. I the exchange continues, he gradually gets worth ignoring my company totally or what I am saying for that matter, he demanded that I sign up and went very personal loose professionalism. On the other hand, I played in his game and kept on referring to this Playbook and he proved himself to be a good fit for it by the account of his performance as you can see.

Written by Trisha Amable – Girlfridayz – Website: https://girlfridayz.com
Girllfridayz number 10358020 girlfriday, girlfridayz^{tm} is a registered trademark in the UK

I will not be using his company for Bitcoin trades soon as I could see how this going to go if he became my account manager as he told me. If he had played it differently and listened to me pay attention to my company and what I say he may have achieved a sale in six months because I am interested in Bitcoin and another opportunity will present itself to me and will be just right for me.

Conversion

C: Conversion refers to converting a prospect into a paying customer in terms of online business it means a prospect browsing your website and purchasing your good or services is conversion. The conversion rate means is the percentage of prospects who take the desired action.

To convert a prospect into paying customer you need to use the 9 Core Assets along with either an upsell, down-sell or cross-sell. This helps with your conversion rate and increases sales by month, and you will see a constant increase in sales by month.

Hence, Conversion marketing refers to tactics that encourage customers to take a specific action, "converting" a person browsing your website into a purchaser of your product or service. (See the latter example: **How I acquire a new customer using the Core Assets** in the lead part of the formula).

To convert a prospect into paying customers here below two strategies that work treat use these strategies in your business to acquire prospects and convert them into paying customers by using the Core Assets in each document which will certainly attract with the right incentive and persuasive content.

The Ultimate Welcome and Thank Letter

Dear use First Name

Thank you for your order, we really appreciate it.

I would like to reiterate what a great decision you have made. Our client's members tell us often the reason why they buy from us and keep on buying.

- Reason 1
- Reason 2
- Reason 3

Add any information that is relevant to their purchase.

New Customer Special offer

As a thank you for becoming a new customer I am always delighted to offer you our new customer special offer,

Detailed the offer here and ensure you put a deadline in the offer.

Written by Trisha Amable – Girlfridayz – Website: https://girlfridayz.com
Girllfridayz number 10358020 girlfriday, girlfridayz™ is a registered trademark in the UK

Thank again name of the person for your order and remember we are a phone call away call us on add your number or you can send us an email add your email if you have any questions or need any help.

Kind Regards,

Your Name
Date

P.S: Remember this special offer will end (add date) on it will be a shame if you miss out on such offers.

In this template letter, you are re-enforcing the relationship with your new customers to keep them buying from you by stating the reason why others buy from you make sure the testimonial you insert is relevant to their purchase.

Add an incentive in the form of an irresistible offer and ensure you add an expiry date. Re-iterate the thank you and mention the person's first name and add your contact details. In the P.S part remind them of the discount expiry date and add the miss-out line.

This template helps keep your new customers and keeping buying from you and from time to time send them offers related to their first purchase or other product of interest that is (cross-sell)

Upsell is a brilliant marketing strategy coupled with the Core Assets works. The process of upselling is persuading a customer to buy something additional or more expensive while the process of cross-selling invites customers to buy related or complementary items. Though often used interchangeably, both offer distinct benefits and can be effective in tandem.

Here is what you'll be interested in...

- ❖ Sales & Marketing proficiency: by using the Core Assets and strategies daily in your marketing you become proficient.

- ❖ Sales Conversion: You will achieve conversion by using tactics and strategy and selling without selling.

- ❖ Systematisation: When you find strategies that work for you systemised it

- ❖ Lead Acquisition: Using the perfect prospect list and doing half of the list you will see an increase in enquiry and lead or creating a member exclusive club with a referral form attach (template below)

Written by Trisha Amable – Girlfridayz – Website: https://girlfridayz.com
Girllfridayz number 10358020 girlfriday, girlfridayz[tm] is a registered trademark in the UK

❖ Customer Satisfaction: Get social proof the more you have the better as it helps buyer decisions.

You could create an exclusive club for your customer this is a strategy which works it helps you acquire leads and customers very fast below is a template that you can duplicate for your business.

Loyalty card reward card as the example demonstrate below and this strategy is not only for the retail industry or restaurant-specificly but can be used for services too.

A loyalty card strategy for service could be if you're a CV company or a typing service company you could say— get your card stamps once your purchase is over £10, if you've fill your card, we give you a free notepad and a pen. The same could be done online create your loyalty program.

If you are a website designer, you could say purchase a website package and get one stamp. If you complete your loyalty card, get a free social media profile creation.

Lead Churning by the dozen exclusive member club template

The name of the business Exclusive Club

Please enter your details below to join the "name of the club" exclusive from time to time we'll send you details of our unique customer's evenings (if restaurant) parties or gifts and other delightful occasions including (Christmas, New year Eve and Easter, your birthday) all these things are only available for our exclusive members.

You will also be entered in our free monthly prize draw to win a "Free whatever you want to offer for one or two". Thank you again for joining the <name of your business>

First Name: (if a couple enter both names)

Last Name:

Address:

Post Code:

Phone including dialling code:

Written by Trisha Amable – Girlfridayz – Website: https://girlfridayz.com
Girllfridayz number 10358020 girlfriday, girlfridayz^{tm} is a registered trademark in the UK

Your Birthday date: D/M/Y

Partner Birthday date: D/M/Y

Who do you know like yourself who appreciates good quality products or services and would like to receive information about the business?

1. First Name   Last Name:

Address

Post Code:

2. First Name   Last Name:

Address

Post Code:

Please note your details are safe with us. We will only use them to send you a notification about the name of the business.

Exclusive club

Creating a member club for your website or your business is the best way to acquire customers and leads plus the form doubles up as a referral form.

You can see that converting customers is easy when you are using the Core Assets in your pitch, and it is part of your conversation it then flows naturally and then you are selling without selling.

On occasion, it is not easy and it can be hard to get money out of people and testimonials alone cannot do the job because when you meet sceptical customers, they need convincing and a bit more even if they are interested in what you are offering, they will automatically want to know more. It is in their DNA so for these customers the Core Assets work, but you need to use different strategies to achieve a sale.

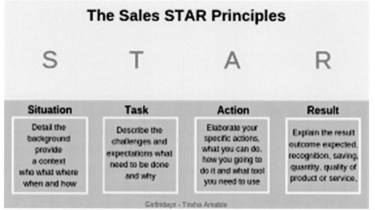

The Sales Star Principles win the heart of your customer with the Wow factor.
Figure 3 The START SALES PRINCIPALES©

Girlfridayz SALES STAR PRINCIPLES®© devised by Patricia Amable of Girlfridayz created on the 13th/04/2019 is a method used in sales to convince customers to purchase your product or service especially if the customer is sceptical and asks you certain questions about your services or products and business.

Girlfridayz SALES STAR PRINCIPLES®© method is a structured manner of responding to behavioural-based customers questions discussing the specific situation, task, action, and result of the situation you are describing and highlighting the benefit the customers will gain using your products or your services in a specific manner relevant to their query and it helps you provide more specific details to satisfy the customers need and to secure a sale.

Girlfridayz SALE STAR PRINCIPALES®© is a sale model based on our own experiences with our customers and prospective customers since starting Girlfridayz and we designed a sale model called SALES STAR PRINCIPLES®© which can help you structure your responses and answer your customers either B2B or B2C with relevant answers to their query either about your business, services, or products.

What are the Girlfridayz SALES STAR PRINCIPALE®©

The Girlfridayz Sales Star Principles® is very simple and is composed of 4 criteria which are:

Situation - Detail the background, provide a context where, when, what, who and How

Task - Describe the challenge and expectation if any and what needs to be done and why.

Action - Elaborate on your specific action, what you need to do, how you going to do it and what tool you need to use.

Result - Explain the resulting outcome expected, recognition, saving, quantity and quality of products or services which justify the price.

Can you see how it is structured, easy to understand and apply to any sales situation when a customer required specific answers to their questions before deciding to purchase your products or services and need to be convinced?

It can be used with any sales strategies such as upsell, cross-sell and down-sell strategies or comparison with your competitor for the same or similar services or products.

Ensure that you stress the benefit of using your service or if it is a product more the benefit of having the product than the features of the product even though the features of a product are as important as the benefit it provides will make its features shine.

When using the Girlfridayz SALES STAR PRINCIPALE® method it is important not to waffles but instead, be relevant and specific to what you are selling, therefore, provide answers related to the products or services that the customers querying about and be knowledgeable about your products or services. **Deliver your product or service like a seasoned pro.**

Written by Trisha Amable – Girlfridayz – Website: https://girlfridayz.com
Girlllfridayz number 10358020 girlfriday, girlfridayz^tm is a registered trademark in the UK

Multiplying Customer Value

M: Multiply customer value refer to automation, subscription, and referral

Automation is making money while you sleep you have an online store full of products and people purchase your product, however, you must deliver the product to the customers unless you sell downloads the delivery is automatically done as it is saved on the person computer.

You can offer a subscription yearly or two years contract with a monthly payment you ensure recurring income monthly.

You can have a referral program such as the example above when I put the ultimate template in the exclusive club membership. You capture leads (the member of your club) and then offer a monthly prize draw first person wins the first prize then the second person wins the second prize and offers something on each celebration day to your member and the referral come from the bottom part of the form when asking if you know anyone which can benefit been a member of the exclusive club.

The picture below explained the 4 sections of Maximising Customer Value when trying to maximise customers' value for your business it reduces attrition, increase the frequency of purchase of your product or services, you are also generating more referral and your average order value increased gradually and steadily.

You can use an autoresponder in your email, and you can use upfront costs such as £10 upfront and the rest of the payment a week before delivery. Or upfront cost £69 their monthly payment and length of contract 1 to 2 years or more.

Automating your process and systemising your strategies and tactics used in your business will maximise your customer value as demonstrated above in the template **Lead Churning by the dozen exclusive member club template.**

A system is a set of things working together as part of a mechanism or an interconnecting network of a complex whole. Any strategies and tactics used in your business systemise the one which is working by using them as a whole and they become part of your business system the how you do things meaning how the business operates.

The 4 Sections of Maximising Customer Value

Are a metric that allows you to devise your customer into 4 quadrants and devised strategies for the customer types and their behavioural purchase pattern of your products or services about your competitor by reducing attrition meaning trying to do a better job than your competitor and see if their customers move to your business by devising an attractive strategy, but do not steal your competitor customers only gentle persuasion is needed to reduce attrition. Frequency of purchase aims to get hourly, daily weekly, monthly, and yearly sales to maximise your income gain. Average value order set your prices to get average prices for your products or services to attract a wide range of customers and prospects as now they

Written by Trisha Amable – Girlfridayz – Website: https://girlfridayz.com
Girllfridayz number 10358020 girlfriday, girlfridayz[tm] is a registered trademark in the UK

see you as an affordable option and you become a real choice amongst the competition. Devise a strategy to get more referrals to your services or product word of mouth is the best referral strategy, do an excellent product or service and word of mouth will get referrals as your customers will not stop talking about you. Even if you are online the opportunities to get referrals is immense via a share of post or tweet, comment under your post, likes and reaction all these can entice people to visit your website because other people like your content so ensure there is always a link inserted in your content to maximise backlink.

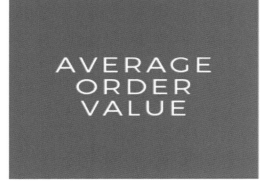

System

S: The S part of the formula refer to systemising the processes such as the exclusive club template if it works it becomes part of your business some you do monthly the prize draw and celebration yearly, capture client and the referral become a system and become part of your business system to acquire leads and paying customer.

A system makes your business grow exponent 3 that is why the formula is $(TxLxCxM)^3$ S = Exponential Growth

You can have a visual representation of the formula let me show it multiplying effect using numbers to use the formula in your business and see your growth put your number.

The third column is your result after applying the T element of the formula transforming your existing sales and marketing and the t & s is your result after using **tactics** and **strategies** and the last column adds more tactics and strategies plus 10%.

Written by Trisha Amable – Girlfridayz – Website: https://girlfridayz.com
Girllfridayz number 10358020 girlfriday, girlfridayz^{tm} is a registered trademark in the UK

The Formula for every SME size business

Component	Current Month	After 15% improvement (DNA)	T&S	After adding more T&S – 10%
L: Generation	200	215	14	220
C: Conversion	30%	31%	13	33%
M: Customer Value	£500	£525	11	£577.50
Total Turnover	£30,000	£34,991 (AVR increase of £32.49 per month	38	£41,926.50 (AVR increase of £35.63 per month

You increase your monthly turnover monthly. In this example, we say we got 200 leads and converted 30% of them and the Average customer value for that month was £500 using the formula it gives you a turnover of £30.000 then after changing transforming our sales and marketing we see an improvement in lead 215 the next month 31% conversion and average customer value £525 then using the formula you increase your turnover by £4991.

You use 14 lead generations tactics & strategies 15 conversion tactics & strategies and 11 customer value tactics and strategies total used 38 in a month the next column you used more tactics and strategies bring 225 and jump to 33% then your customer value increases to £577.50 you add 10% then using the formula you increase your turnover by £6935.50.

Defining what is success in business.

Business success is not the amount of profit a business makes the profit is the result of the system implemented in your business therefore it is the result of using the formula which determines your business profitability. Because you only acquire profit by deducting all costs associated with the business the money left is your profit.

Therefore, a business is deemed successful when all the right systems are in place and make the business run like a good oil machine which never stops as you keep on oiling, so it performs to its maximum capability, it is the processes used in your business which make your business successful. The outcome of these processes is the money your business is making, and it only becomes profitable when it outweighs its cost.

This playbook gives you the right foundation and helps you engineer visible growth as your sales and marketing will be improved using the technique and method highlighted in this playbook.

Work hard lay the right foundation, model, and implement what the best are doing you will then enter the right condition for success. Implement the tactic in this playbook and you will

Written by Trisha Amable – Girlfridayz – Website: https://girlfridayz.com
Girllfridayz number 10358020 girlfriday, girlfridayz[tm] is a registered trademark in the UK

notice an increase in sales of your product or service. You will notice an increase in lead acquisition and an increase in profit over time. The business growth you will experience is not tangible but visible as you will have implemented the right system in your business.

Work assiduously and apply the tactics & strategies in this playbook and develop new strategies based on the strategies in this playbook. This playbook contains workable strategies which produce result over time the power of your business growth is in its system and the system take care of them for you.

Focus on the clientele and ensure you provide value to your customers as well as an answer to their needs. Capture customer details other than their email as email does not permit you to automate your strategy and tactic use, but permit you to send information about your business, product, or services.

Focus on the clientele's effective Sale letter that works for B2B template (TM)

Customer details

Out of sight, out of mind? Make sure Your Customers Don't Forget You during the holiday season (H)

Dear Name of person

Summer is picking up speed and so is the holiday season, many of your customers and business partners will be taking a few weeks off from their daily work. Make sure they don't forget your company by presenting them with long-lasting, high-quality personalised promotional gifts The Crown Triple Function Pen. (RW) to ensure that your company name logo will remain at the front of their mind even during their holiday.

Order your Crown Triple Function Pen today (CTA)

- High-quality metal pen
- Metallic Soft-Touch-Finish   Features
- Bright LED flashlight at the end of the barrel
- Stylus on the lid

Personalisation in a standard font at no extra cost and available in other colours. (B)

The sale letter template continues below

4 easy ways to order:

- Online at your website
- Call us your number and email us at your@business.com
- Mail using the enclosed postage paid envelope   Benefit
- Fax your fax

Whatever the time of the year, your business name personalised gift is an easy way and affordable way to set yourself apart from the competition (D). Choose **your business name** to promote your company and be noticed, remember, and talked about. (RW)

Yours sincerely,

Your name and title

PS: Remember, **your business name** 100% satisfaction guarantee means that if you are not completely satisfied with your purchase you can return it to us for a full refund within 14 days of purchase (G)

---detached order form here ------------------------------------

Order Now -This offer expires in 30 days (IO & CTA)

In this section add your order form with offer details, all your condition and payment options and ensure you got a section for customers to add payment card detail or send a cheque or if they prefer an invoice. The order form attached is only for the product mentioned in the letter.

At the end of the form say how you going to process the customer data and if you going to use that data to send them an advert and an opt-out option (in a small font but visible)

TO ORDER BY PHONE, CALL **YOUR NUMBER** OR FAX THE ORDER FORM TO **YOUR FAX NUMBER (CTA)**

This template is best used for the cross-selling strategy for existing customers noticed that in the template **I am pushing only 1 product using 8 core elements to maximise order for this product in this sale letter template.**

There is no social proof but if you want to add more weight and you have customers who use this product or order from you before adds one or two testimonial and your sale letter will be using the 9-Core Assets of marketing.

Why do I say this mighty Sale Letter is good for cross-selling because if you are a company which provides personalise giveaway items as the example used in this sale letter template you have sold previously to your customer a diary or pen you can cross-sell them with another pen or any other personalised item you have?

The same template sale letter can be used for B2C customers with the same strategy and tactics to make more effective personalised items for your customers only.

By attaching an order form to the letter with a self-address stamped envelope you are securing fast ordering as the customer can order directly from the letter and send you payment hence easy conversion.

Adding an order form to a letter is a conversion strategy combined with the content of the sale letter using 8 or 9 tactics is a sure workable effective template which gets you results.

41

Written by Trisha Amable – Girlfridayz – Website: https://girlfridayz.com
Girllfridayz number 10358020 girlfriday, girlfridayz^tm is a registered trademark in the UK

This template can be systemised and part of your business system and provide value to the customer by providing useful information about the product and 4 easy ways to order therefore no hassle to the customers as every preferred method to order is featured in this letter, including a self-address stamped envelope and no further cost to the customer apart paying for their order.

You can use this template sale letter with a prospective customer and push only one product you choose your target market then set the content using at least 8 or 9 tactics and adds an order form and there you go conversion straight off if the prospect like the product you are pushing, they can buy straight away.

Do not attach a long lengthy order form but a short order form containing all the information mentioned above. Preferably point 10 in a word document. This template is effective with or without a picture of the product and social proof, but it is more effective with a picture of the product, or you can add a sample of the product in the letter which can help increase conversion rates.

Implement this mighty effective sale letter and you will notice an increase in sales by month.

Digital Pull and reach using the Core Assets.

The Core Assets and the strategy above can be used in a post on social media platforms mainly Facebook because you got the opportunity to write lengthy concise content using the 9 tactics and strategies to sell a product or a service with the right technique and method. The power words are called keywords and longtail are used to find you on a search engine so even if you use Social Media Platforms to promote your products or services remember to use the formula and combine it with strategies. Market research conducted by Amable — found that 90% of organisations state that their organisation will focus more on data from new sources such as social media (Amable, 2017).

On LinkedIn, if your customers are B2B use the Core Assets and the strategies in your post as LinkedIn permits you to do so. Write concisely because there's a content length for a post therefore by learning to write concisely you become proficient and you produce better content which attracts potential customers and will result in sales with the people who are interested in what you have to offer.

Effective Social Media Post Template for a Service

Starting a business can be daunting without the right help (H)

Post body content

When you start up a business you need a Business Plan because it is a structured manner to write your ideas about your business. When you write your idea in a business plan you start noticing your business concept coming to life in a clear and structured way. (TM, RW, B)

Written by Trisha Amable – Girlfridayz – Website: https://girlfridayz.com
Girllfridayz number 10358020 girlfriday, girlfridayz[tm] is a registered trademark in the UK

Starting a business without a plan you set yourself to fail. With a business plan, you are guaranteed to increase your chance of success because you see your business goals and how to execute them. (TM, D, G)

As a start-up business it may be difficult for you to structure your business plan at [add business name] we offer free advice on starting a Business Plan which attracts lenders to give you start-up funding. (IO)

Call us on [add your number] or access free advice via your website [insert link] (CTA)

This post is effective as am pushing only one service and using 8 Core Assets to target people who want to start a business or started a business without a plan this post will attract both groups of people. This post on Facebook will be highly effective to target these groups because Facebook offers the possibility of geo-targeting people in a specific category therefore this template post will get you results as you will only send it to the TM highlighted in the headline and the post body content.

This template is multipurpose because it scopes not only lie with Facebook it can be used in email marketing on LinkedIn but remember LinkedIn does not have much segmentation so you can be limited in geo-targeting the group mentioned in the template. However, LinkedIn has groups so join a group about your business and post using this template.

If you are a Twitter fan you can tweet using the 8 Core Assets of marketing however, due to the length of tweets permitted by Twitter you need to add supporting media to achieve your aim. But bear in mind there is no segmentation hence your chance of success relies on someone being interested in your tweets.

Effective Tweet template using 8 Core Assets and one strategy.

You cannot have a headline to push a product on Tweeter however, on Tweeter you can use your Headline as a tweet if it is powerful enough to generate interest with a CTA and back it up with a video or picture.

This template below pushes a service and it's a Business Plan.

Tweet body content

Starting a business without a plan you set yourself to fail. With a business plan, you are guaranteed to increase your chance of success because you see your business goals and how to execute them. Get free advice [phone or website link] (TM, D, G, CTA)

This template is 221 characters up to free advice so your CTA will not fit unless it's 7 characters in length to overcome this add a picture with your details and the picture have your offer where to get the advice. You can use an infographic about your service in the template we trying to get more Business Plan order so an infographic with the business detail can lead to conversion please see an example of an infographic which feature the rest of the Core Assets needed to try to generate lead and eventual conversion via Twitter.

Written by Trisha Amable – Girlfridayz – Website: https://girlfridayz.com
Girllfridayz number 10358020 girlfriday, girlfridayz[tm] is a registered trademark in the UK

H, RW, D, B, CTA, IO

Are present in this infographic.

Using social media get you lead and conversion, but it does matter how you do it, you need to segment your market and post in the pertaining group of interest to increase your chance to acquire. Your best chances are on Facebook and then LinkedIn after and the least is Twitter because Twitter is based on the chance that someone is interested in your content but if you demark your group of interest your chance increased drastically to acquire lead due to the possibility of segmenting your reach.

Email Marketing

Email Marketing your title can be the winning combination which makes the receiver of your email pay attention and read the body content which should match your title information. Meaning that your title should feature in the body content not word by word but enough for your reader to recognise what you are talking about. Your email title serves as the opening for your content, the body is the main jest of your information which should be separated by a clear paragraph. Every paragraph should follow each other, and your ending paragraph

44

Written by Trisha Amable – Girlfridayz – Website: https://girlfridayz.com
Girllfridayz number 10358020 girlfriday, girlfridayz[tm] is a registered trademark in the UK

concludes your information and lead to your CTA (Call to Action). A CTA is a short directional text which tells your reader the action you want them to perform.

We have written 7 ways to write a winning email subject line which should support you to write a winning email title which will increase your click-through rate and acquisition of prospects and eventually customers.

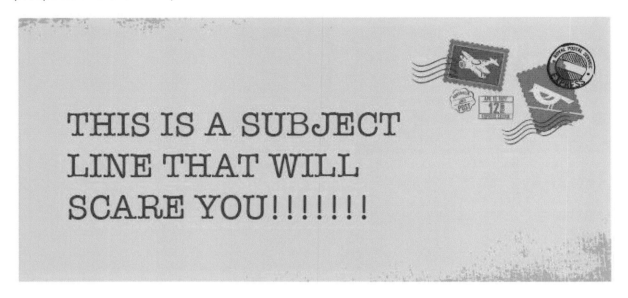

7 Ways to Writing a Winning Email Subject Line

In the digital age, having your business stand out is harder than ever. What used to be a few flyers on your doorstep is now an overflowing email inbox. This difference is not to be overlooked when creating your marketing plan Girlfridayz has a great marketing plan plus a guide for you to download and complete. A great email can go a long way in building your clientele and growing your brand.

While there is no one formula for creating compelling emails, an undeniable fact is that your email won't be read if it isn't opened. That is why your email subject line needs to grab your reader's attention from the get-go.

Get your newsletters in front of a captive audience by following these dynamite tips for writing a winning subject line. Newsletters are a great vehicle to promote your business with informative and valuable for your reader. If done correctly you can build followers and ambassadors for your business, increase prospects and it can lead to customers.

Change Is Good

Make sure that your subject line is different each time. This lets your recipient know that there is a person behind the screen and the conversation is natural. It also means you will be more specific about what is in the body of the email, piquing your readers' curiosity. And curiosity is an excellent marketing strategy combined with the Core Assets of marketing to create a wave of queries and customers for your business.

45

Written by Trisha Amable – Girlfridayz – Website: https://girlfridayz.com
Girllfridayz number 10358020 girlfriday, girlfridayz™ is a registered trademark in the UK

Numbers Matter

With over 50% of people browsing through mobile devices, long titles are a thing of the past. Smaller screens call for shorts and compact text that can be easily read without getting cut off. When writing your subject line, use 50 characters or less. This is a cold hard rule. Whenever possible, try to stick with as few words as possible (ideally 28-39).

Who Are You?

Keep the "From" line consistent and clear. This will help readers contextualize your email right away. They will be reassured that the email is not spam, but a requested mail more tailored to their interests. To maintain strong branding as your company grows, we recommend using the name of your company rather than that of an individual.

DO YOU WANT TO READ ME?!?!

Writing a question can work wonders but all CAPS or lots of !!! won't help your brand. Devise a question that makes a reader want to say "yes" or "I want to know more". Also, when doing promotional emails, still be careful to appeal to the individual on an interesting, informative, and emotional level. **For example**: "Want to make a splash at your summer party?" or "When's the last time you slept like a log?" – Emotion is a strong marketing strategy, and you increase your customers by 30% easy as you draw them in with content they can relate to, therefore drawn to it naturally.

Avoid Triggers

Try not to use words that trigger spam filters. You'll want to avoid – free, help, % off, sale, and donate. This way your email will stay in your users' general inbox rather than the dreaded spam or promotions section or be deleted because people are sick and tired to receive the same title from many companies and some will automatically delete it without reading or remain in their inbox and never viewed and eventually deleted. Hence, keep your title interesting.

Tell Don't Sell

It is best to remain casual, the same way you would communicate with a friend or colleague (just with a proofreader). Tell your readers about your new offer rather than making an immediate sales pitch. That said, make sure to maintain proper grammar and a professional tone because you are representing your brand and if people perceive you as unprofessional, they will not use you but your competitors.

Having said that it is not always the case but do not take chances in thinking your grammar mistakes do not matter as it is not a comfortable place to ignore them, and you need to make every effort to correct them to increase your chances of selling.

Written by Trisha Amable – Girlfridayz – Website: https://girlfridayz.com
Girllfridayz number 10358020 girlfriday, girlfridayz^{tm} is a registered trademark in the UK

The Conversation Is Two-Sided

Indicate if you need a response. If the body of your email is offering something for a limited time, or if you are hosting an event requiring an RSVP, let your readers know in the subject line. This will encourage them to open the email right away rather than get to it at the end of the week, perhaps when the opportunity has already passed.

After incorporating these suggestions into your email marketing plan, you can begin to test them out. Track your open rate and see if you find patterns of what is working for you as market testing is very important as if you find the one subject line which gets you results systemised the subject line.

Here are 5 email templates which can start you off in writing a winning email.

PRODUCT EMAIL TEMPLATE

Subject Line: Should introduce Product name (Get the latest iPhone RS and be the envy of your friend)

Hey, [Name],

[One-sentence benefit of new feature] (H)

[Introduction of the product] (RW)

Here's how it works:

(Explain how it work and the benefit and feature of the product) (FB) (D) (G)

[Image of the product]

[#1 tip for using the product with inserted CTA]

If you have any questions, just reply to this email.

[Name] from [Company]

BLOG UPDATE EMAIL TEMPLATE

[Headline]: How to win 10 clients in 30 days [Blog Post]

[Feature image]

[Here's what you'll learn from the post: bullet points or a summary] (FB)

[Read post (CTA)]

[Popular post links]

Written by Trisha Amable – Girlfridayz – Website: https://girlfridayz.com
Girllfridayz number 10358020 girlfriday, girlfridayz™ is a registered trademark in the UK

DISCOUNT OFFER EMAIL TEMPLATE

Headline: We have an irresistible offer for you based on your recent purchase

Hey [Name],

[One sentence offer] (IO)

[GIF or image of the product(s) on offer]

Here's how it works: (FB, RW, D, G)

What's on offer?

How to claim the offer

When does the offer expire?

[Product Link]

[Terms and Conditions link]

REVIEW PROMPT EMAIL TEMPLATE

Subject Line: We want to thank you for purchasing [insert product name]

[Thanks for your purchase]

[Incentive for leaving a review] (RW and IO)

[Leave a review CTA]

[Customer service information or FAQs link]

Here's an example of a good review request email

This email example is great because it:

- Tells the buyer why you want a review.
- Encourages participation by offering entry into a prize draw.
- Has a big review link to make it obvious where to leave a review?
- These reviews are then featured on your homepage to show new visitors that they can trust the brand:

Dear [person name]

Thank you for your recent purchase from [insert company]

To improve the satisfaction of our customers, we have partnered with the online review community, Trustpilot, to collect reviews,

Written by Trisha Amable – Girlfridayz – Website: https://girlfridayz.com
Girllfridayz number 10358020 girlfriday, girlfridayz™ is a registered trademark in the UK

Every review that is submitted will be entered in a prize draw for the chance to win a free [your product name], each month, [prize] will be given away to Trustpilot reviewers.

We are committed to always providing exceptional service. If you have any problems with your product purchased or the delivery of the product, please contact our customer services team at support@companyname.com before leaving a review, and they will resolve any problem for you.

Click here to review us on Trustpilot.

Put a picture of Trustpilot grading.

All reviews, good, bad, or otherwise will be visible immediately.

Thanks for your time and consideration.

Best Regards

Your company name team

Website URL details

ABANDONED CART EMAIL TEMPLATE

[Headline: Did you forget something? /You left something behind]

[Product description and image]

[Continue shopping CTA]

[Reasons to buy from your company]

36 Email subject lines that work a charm and churn lead with open rates.

Outreach customers and prospects with these 35 email subject template and increase your reach without clogging up your prospect mailbox. If you overflow your prospects' mailbox your open rate will suffer and end up in the deleted piles of emails received without being read. Hence to increase your chances use them moderately at a reasonable frequency of sending emails to your clients or prospects.

1. THE CO-PROMOTION OPPORTUNITY EMAIL

Subject line: {Your Company} / {Direct Competitor Company} co-promotion opportunity

Open rate: 60%

This subject line works well because it is short, lightly personalized, and makes an offer right off the bat — "co-promotion opportunity." It is a little vague, which works well because it piques interest enough to get the prospect to click through.

Written by Trisha Amable – Girlfridayz – Website: https://girlfridayz.com
Girllfridayz number 10358020 girlfriday, girlfridayz™ is a registered trademark in the UK

Co-promotion is a marketing practice that permits two or more companies in the same industry to join forces to promote a product or service under the same brand and price with a single marketing strategy. It is considered a form of joint marketing (Kaib, 1988).

You can use this strategy in your niche with your direct competitor if you have a similar size audience that your direct competitor and it does not matter if your brand is well known. This strategy is a win-win if executed rightly and the body of the email explains the co-promotion offer opportunity explicitly and benefit gain for both companies.

2. THE PARTNERSHIP EMAIL

Subject line: Collaborate? 🏢

Open rate: 69%

This one-word subject line is straightforward in its proposition and arouses curiosity in your prospect the emoji give up a friendly tone and has the potential to increase opened rate. It's like sending an email to one of your buddies with a professional tone as your email body requesting a partnership opportunity in your niche and target audience.

3. THE BEST GUEST BLOGGER EMAIL

Subject line: ✍️ We'd love to be your writer for a day, {Name/CompanyName}!

Open rate: 45%

This subject line is direct and outlines what you want in a friendly tone and uses an outbound technique with a touch of personalisation the emoji emphasised the subject's point of contact. You can use this to collaborate on content with another company's blog.

4. THE JEDI SALES EMAIL

Subject line: {FirstName}, Luke Skywalker wants you to make sales!

Open rate: 64%

This subject line uses humour in its subject and references a movie that many can relate to and has a value proposal and personalisation. Funny references and humour marketing work a charm with your audience but must be used with considerable skill and the audience must feel that it is natural.

Find funny references that naturally make sense to your audience and get creative to make a more memorable first impression. Make sure you have a clear value proposition that is relevant to your audience.

THE SHAMELESS BRIBE

Subject line: Question about Pontin and I'll buy you a cake 🎂.

Open rate: 75%

Written by Trisha Amable – Girlfridayz – Website: https://girlfridayz.com
Girllfridayz number 10358020 girlfriday, girlfridayz[tm] is a registered trademark in the UK

This subject line works because reciprocal marketing works and you inform your prospect in exchange for an answer to my question you get a free cake and the use of the emoji emphasises your offer. The offer is generous, but it stands out because it's infused with a little more humour than your usual cold email. Use a variation of this to collect user feedback on your product and send your offer to the recipient.

6. THE FOMO EMAIL

Subject lines: It helps Startups / Stay ahead of the competition.

Open rate: 52% / 44%

These subject lines compel the recipient to click on the email for two reasons out of fear they may miss out on an opportunity, or they need the information and requested support. it works if it's targeted and solves a problem your recipient has.

This works if the body of your email explained how your product or services can meet the need of the recipient or answer the specific question the recipient asked you with your product or services. to pitch your product/solution if you know your audience's pain point and you can offer something that will work to resolve it.

7. THE "IT'S NOT RUDE TO INVITE YOURSELF AS A GUEST" EMAIL

Subject line: {FirstName}, I Have a Story for You

Open rate: 78%

This subject line works because it uses curiosity marketing and people are generally curious (especially when it involves them). This subject line works because it mentions the recipient and instantly creates intrigue.

This can be used to invite yourself as a guest on a podcast or an event or to promote your content. Only use it if you have something interesting to say and real value to add.

8. THE CUNNING EMAIL

Subject line: Happy w/ {Tool Name}, {First Name}??

Open rate: 71%

This subject line works because it has two layers of personalization; it has the tool name the recipient is using (or used in the past) and their name. It also has a straightforward question that can spark meaningful conversation. It is based on a nostalgia marketing strategy to reach out to your competitor's audience to build relationships, get information to improve your product, or pitch your product if you feel like it can better serve the recipients, you can use it to offer an upgraded version of your product or similar product than the recipient have or had.

9. THE SNACK EMAIL

Subject lines: Tesco {company Name} — Let's get {Company Name} snacking.

Written by Trisha Amable – Girlfridayz – Website: https://girlfridayz.com
Girllfridayz number 10358020 girlfriday, girlfridayz™ is a registered trademark in the UK

Subject lines: iPhone 11 Pro — Let's get {Company Name} snacking.

Subject lines: New marketplace built for businesses — Interested?

Open rate: 52% / 75%

The first and second subject line explains the purpose of the email right away and the second has a witty tone playing with the brand name, it's lightly personalized, and it lets the recipient know who they're coming from. It builds instant credibility if the recipient is familiar with the brand.

The second subject line sparks curiosity. It is intriguing enough not to sound too sales-y, but it hits the right strings of the person receiving the email — who does not want a better solution to anything they are doing?

10. THE I NOTICED YOU NOTICED ME EMAIL

Subject line: You may be interested to improve your SEO {Your Company} because we have noticed some duplicated pages on your {Company Name} website.

Open rate: 92%

This subject line is sniper-targeted at prospects who have visited your website. How do you identify website visitors? You use a tool like Albacross to turn anonymous web traffic into B2B leads and match them with companies in a database to then find their email address. Use this subject line to build relationships with people who are potentially interested in your company.

11. THE CLASSIC QUICK Q EMAIL

Subject line: {FirstName} {Last Name} — Quick Question

Open rate: 76%

This is a very personal email subject suggesting that you know the recipient and the CTA in this subject line arouses interest, making the recipient wonder what the question will be.

12. THE DIRECT Q EMAIL

Subject line: How many people in your team work remotely?

Open rate: N/A

This subject line could not be any clearer or more direct. It is extremely easy for the recipient to reply, and it is a great opener for a follow-up.

13. THE ME + YOU EMAIL

Subject line: {Company Name} + Auto close

Open rate: 48%

Written by Trisha Amable – Girlfridayz – Website: https://girlfridayz.com
Girllfridayz number 10358020 girlfriday, girlfridayz[tm] is a registered trademark in the UK

Once you link a prospect's name with your company, it gets them to open and read the first sentence which needs to be carefully crafted to keep them interested from the get-go. You need to be a brand your audience recognizes for this to be effective.

14. THE "WE'LL GET YOU BETTER RESULTS" EMAIL

Subject line: How happy are you with {Company Name}'s Google Ad performance?

Open rate: N/A

This subject line works because it's relevant to the recipient and it's sent from a credible company that is known to get great results but even if you know to get a great result for others do not assume that the recipient will be receptive therefore your email body must be solution orientated after you have highlighted what you could do better than your competitor.

15. THE MYSTERY EMAIL

Subject line: {Domain Name}.com???

Open rate: 62%

It is human nature to own things, and people are possessive over the stuff they own. This subject line plays with this aspect of human psychology and piques the reader's interest this what call psychology marketing. People like a little mystery. This subject line makes the recipient wonder what could be wrong with their domain name to pique the recipient's interest and emphasizes it with the triple question mark.

16. THE SHOCK & AWE EMAIL

Subject line: OMG {FirstName}

Open rate: 73%

This subject line plays on your recipient's curiosity. If they do not miss it in their inbox, it's almost certain they'll be compelled to click. It is slightly clickbait-y, but you can awe your recipient in the body and show you have done your homework or have a reveal. This subject line is audience specific i.e.: film lover, book lover etc it is designed to get your recipient's attention. What you do with it is up to you — the possibilities are endless.

17. THE CHIMP EMAIL

Subject line: Mailchimp at {Company Name}

Open rate: 68%

This subject line is targeted at companies that use Mailchimp for their email marketing. Hence, it is relevant, comes across as personal, and is intriguing enough for the recipient to open. This tactical subject line is best used if you want to compare your services against the company customers you are targeting and offer a better service to interest them in changing suppliers.

Written by Trisha Amable – Girlfridayz – Website: https://girlfridayz.com
Girllfridayz number 10358020 girlfriday, girlfridayz^{tm} is a registered trademark in the UK

18. THE ENCHILADA EMAIL

Subject line: {FirstName} listen to business and enchiladas podcast.

Subject Line {FirstName} I see you as a guest on business and enchiladas podcast.

Subject Line (FirstName} you be a good fit for business and enchiladas podcast.

Subject Line {FirstName} Podcasting opportunity

Open rate: 82%

These subject lines are straightforward ways to invite people to listen to your podcast and the other one to invite them as a guest on your podcast you could also ask an invite question in the same style. The last subject line suggests that the body of the email has the podcast title opportunity offer.

19. THE TIRE PUMP EMAIL

Subject line: We set the stage for {Company Name} to be the talk of {Location} 💥

Open rate: 86%

This is an attention-grabbing subject line with two layers of personalization — name and location. It is highly targeted to prospects who are looking to grow their business and aroused curiosity with the irresistible offer that they cannot refuse therefore the body must be juicy enough to keep the recipient interested.

20. THE APOLOGETIC INTERRUPTER EMAIL

Subject line: Apologies in advance, {FirstName}

Open rate: 26%

Given that you are sending a cold email, prospects will see the subject and wonder "Why is a stranger apologizing to me?"

It takes what is normally a disadvantage (being an unknown quantity) and turns it into an advantage (you raise the prospect's curiosity, and they open your email). Then it's down to the rest of your email to entertain and maintain their attention. It has a clickbait intonation to it and can be a risky strategy and has a tone of dishonesty and could put off the recipient. Add a small element of personalization to this subject line, like {FirstName}, to maximize its potential.

21. THE I ACKNOWLEDGE YOUR EMAIL

Subject line: Congrats on {Something Noteworthy} {FirstName}

Open rate: 46%

Written by Trisha Amable – Girlfridayz – Website: https://girlfridayz.com
Girllfridayz number 10358020 girlfriday, girlfridayz^{tm} is a registered trademark in the UK

The classic email (congrats/love your work) works wonders if you are skilful at using it. In all honesty, it can sound a little spammy if not done correctly. The strategy comes down to two things: timing and relevance and genuine appreciation of the achievement.

This is the beginning of selling without selling as the recipient will respond to you and your second email should be conversational but do not talk about your service or product until asked.

You can achieve a sale or enquiry about your services or be referred to the recipient associate or friends who might need your services or products if you are patient, friendly and professional all these should happen at any given time.

Never try to sell something in the first email with this subject line and to do this successfully you have researched your prospect so you are knowledgeable about them and you found that they may be a good candidate for your services or products.

22. THE CLASSIC COLD OUTREACH EMAIL

Subject line: Hey {FirstName}, I have a question about {Company Name}

Open rate: 80%

This one is a standard outreach email, but it has more personalization, which makes it a lot more effective than the usual spammy mass outreach email.

23. THE REMINDER EMAIL

Subject line: I saw you were at {Relevant Location} too, I have a question.

Open rate: 75%

This subject line exploits a mutual experience to create relevancy and pique the interest of the reader you could use this if you met someone at a business event or launch party etc or if you met them at the grocery store and had a brief casual discussion and they gave you, their details.

24. THE SERENADE EMAIL

Subject line: I just called to say I like you.

Open rate: 52%

This subject line is a little cheesy. But pop song references make things fun and more personable. This strategy is used to follow up on a cold call that was rejected but before you use anything like this you do your research on your prospect and what they really or dislike. If you manage to find something of their interest you use it to your advantage, and you might achieve a successful sale.

Written by Trisha Amable – Girlfridayz – Website: https://girlfridayz.com
Girllfridayz number 10358020 girlfriday, girlfridayz[tm] is a registered trademark in the UK

25. THE DIPLOMATIC EMAIL

Subject line: Editorial Inquiry

Open rate: 70%

This subject line sounds a little dry and political. But it works because it's clear and direct and it is audience specific only.

26. THE ADVISOR'S EMAIL

Subject line: Freelancer Advice

Open rate: 62%

This subject line is targeted and direct, but vague enough to pique the recipient's interest to open the email and read the first sentence.

27. THE PUNCHLINE EMAIL

Subject Line: Re: Fake subject line to get your attention.

Subject Line: Re: Fake news which may interest you

Open Rate: 55%

This strategy use humour and the re: is tricking the reader into opening your email. However, this subject line admits that it is trickery immediately. It is like a mini joke in the subject line. People can get a hearty chuckle, and then they open your email. Then it's up to the rest of your email to entertain and maintain their attention."

28. THE FEAR-INDUCING EMAIL

Subject line: The top ten reasons you will fail.

Open rate: 47%

People will move faster to avoid pain than to seek pleasure. This subject line plays with that basic premise of human psychology and forces the recipient to open your email out of fear. You need to research your prospect for it to be effective and work better with Introverts and extroverts (people who have introvert and extrovert personality traits). The body of the email must be explicit and bear the tone of the subject line. Use with caution otherwise, it can backfire, and you may receive negative press.

29. THE FEAR-INDUCING EMAIL

Subject Line: The top ten reasons why businesses fail

Open rate: 70%

This subject line plays with that basic premise of human psychology and forces the recipient to open your email out of fear even if the subject is factual and it has a high open rate due to

Written by Trisha Amable – Girlfridayz – Website: https://girlfridayz.com
Girllfridayz number 10358020 girlfriday, girlfridayz™ is a registered trademark in the UK

this fact the body of the email you be also factual and informative for the recipient to be interested.

30. THE PLEASURE-INDUCING EMAIL

Subject Line: 10 reasons you are destined to succeed.

Open rate: 80%

People love pleasure and positive input and will open your email as it generates interest in the reader. It is not cheesy or clickbait-y, but your email body must be explicitly and informative about the area of success that the recipient will gain following your advice.

31. THE SNIPER-TARGETED EMAIL

Subject line: VR and 360 Storytelling

Open rate: 63%

This subject line might not make sense because it's not contextualized. But it's the principles behind it that make it so effective. Its sniper targeted the recipient and was extremely relevant and contextual. Your email body must be explicit and interesting enough to keep your recipient entertained.

32. THE CLASSIC CHECK-IN EMAIL

Subject line: {Company Name} Check-in

Open rate: 57%

This subject line is only slightly deceiving. Check-in implies the sender has a relationship with the recipient. However, it works well to get your email opened. Because it involves some level of trickery, make sure you have something of immense value to add to the recipient.

33. THE ONE-SHOT EMAIL

Subject line: Was on {Company Name}'s Website, and I have one question!

Subject Line: {FirstName} I was on {Company Name}'s Website, and I have one question!

Open rate: 52%

You only have one shot. One opportunity. This is a classic outreach email. Make sure you have ONE question and don't get all sales-y your question refers to the content seen on the company website if you have identified a problem and you can provide a solution to fix it. This is to be used skilfully and the recipient may reply we have a deal offer for your company.

34. THE OPEN-ENDED Q EMAIL

Subject line: What's next for {Company Name}?

Open rate: 62%

Written by Trisha Amable – Girlfridayz – Website: https://girlfridayz.com
Girllfridayz number 10358020 girlfriday, girlfridayz™ is a registered trademark in the UK

This subject line works because it is direct, yet open-ended. It is a solid way to spark conversation and start building a relationship with your prospect.

35. THE WARM COLD EMAIL

Subject line: This email should be in your spam {FirstName} but…

Open rate: 87%

Despite this being a cold email, the fact that it lands in the prospect's inbox creates some credibility with the recipient and piques their interest enough to open and read the first sentence for some context as it has a humourist and curiosity tone therefore the content should match the tone of the email subject this tactic require marketing skills.

36. THE QUICKIE EMAIL

Subject line: Quick Read

Subject Line: Quick Makeup Tips

Subject Line: Must Have

Open rate: 52%

This is a classic cold outreach subject line that works because of its brevity and clarity. It is also very audience and niche specific. You need to have built a following in whatever you provide meaning your audiences know you and they will respond favourably to these short subject lines.

These subject line templates are used by pros marketers and have all been tried and tested and they work, however, apart from the subject line, many factors will affect the open rates of your email, including your brand's reputation, credibility, and targeting.

You will need to conduct customer and prospect research for some of the subject line templates before you use them as their very personalised and very targeted and requires considerable skills and knowledge to be effective and work to your advantage.

You will need to A/B split test the audience niche-related subject line with your following to find out which one works the best and you could create more of your bases on your niche and your industry and your audience taste.

It takes work to do it right, but the results are worth it. It all comes down to how much effort you are willing to put in.

Some subject Line makes use of Digital Psychology which is the combination of behavioural economics and psychology. Examples of digital psychology in the subject lines above are:

❖ External triggers like call-to-actions that you can have in your subject line.

❖ Internal triggers like FOMO make your prospect act out of fear of missing an opportunity.

Written by Trisha Amable – Girlfridayz – Website: https://girlfridayz.com
Girllfridayz number 10358020 girlfriday, girlfridayz™ is a registered trademark in the UK

- ❖ Loss aversion: people move faster to avoid pain than to seek pleasure. Use this to get your prospect to act.

- ❖ Rewards: everybody likes rewards and appreciation. It releases dopamine. Flatter your prospect. But do not overdo it and be too cheesy.

- ❖ Shameless corruption: gift people with cakes and other shiny things.

10 effective marketing strategies small businesses rarely used.

Marketing a small business is not that easy and competing against the larger businesses to have a share of your niche can be a struggle due to lack of funding, staffing, and the constant changing face of marketing. However, marketing changing its attire constantly in our fast-paced society one may have forgotten the basic but very efficient marketing strategy used for a century. Community involvement, Community networking, and a little kindness go a long way,

Send handwritten letters with a photo.

It may sound a bit mad. time-consuming and you might be worried about mistakes, you might be right, but you be wrong not to try this technique. Most small businesses are content with typewritten letters, and expensive, high-gloss marketing mailings.

Maybe you can try a different approach. Go on a note-writing spree, find a relevant message to share with your community, and include a photo of your family, your small business location, your team, or you at work.

And do not forget to smile!

Sponsor your local kid school event.

What do kids love? Bouncing castles, balloons, sweets, games and cakes. What do parents love? Taking their kids to the events for free. What are you waiting for? Attend your local kid school cake sale, bring your cake, mingle with the parents, and school staff, and give free stuff to the school such as donations of old toys or clothes.

Host a community party.

Why is it that residential neighbourhoods get to have all the fun? Get your small business in party mode. You can start a party wherever you are. Invite other local businesses, rent a barbecue, prepare some free soft drinks, and have some fun! If you are lucky, you might even get some news coverage!

Written by Trisha Amable – Girlfridayz – Website: https://girlfridayz.com
Girllfridayz number 10358020 girlfriday, girlfridayz^{tm} is a registered trademark in the UK

Give stuff away.

You like going to McDonald and Costa coffee not just for the food or the coffee but also for the free Wi-Fi they offer whether you are a customer or not you can just log into their Wi-Fi for free, but while you are there you are using their internet connection for free you might develop a thirst and hunger so you opt-in and purchase coffee and cake or burger fries and drink.

If these giveaway strategies were not working, they would have stopped a long time ago. But each of these for-profit businesses is still thriving and still giving away something of value for free to anyone a profit maker.

Try this.

Find speaking engagements.

- Another connective point between your brand and your business brand is public speaking.
- If public speaking simply is not your thing, you can skip to the next section. If I caught your attention, then here are my tips:
- Start by speaking at community colleges. Many small schools are eager to hear from local businesspeople, especially if your skillset and experience are relevant to a class.
- Submit pitches. Submit a speaking pitch for local events and conferences.
- Become a sponsor for local conferences. Often, the reward for your sponsorship is a brief speaking session about your business.
- Get involved in community groups and clubs. Most organisations are not posting speaking opportunities online. You must be connected to find the opportunities.
- Just ask. Find a well-connected person and ask them about speaking opportunities. And if you do not know any well-connected people, your local library may be a suitable starting place.

Get involved in a community cause.

Pick one worthy cause to get excited about and go do it. Your business can become the go-to champion for cleaning up the Thames, donating blood, combating homelessness offering your service at the food bank, protecting animals, recycling old computers, or building more green spaces.

When a business develops a passion for the community, it fosters a sense of goodwill and respect.

Your personal brand matters just as much as — if not more than — your business brand. By expanding your personal role in the community, you can help grow your business.

Written by Trisha Amable – Girlfridayz – Website: https://girlfridayz.com
Girllfridayz number 10358020 girlfriday, girlfridayz[tm] is a registered trademark in the UK

Place your business logo and contact information on your vehicle.

You might be surprised at the kind of visibility you will get when you put your phone number on your vehicle. People might be curious and give you a call. Drivers might be bored and give you a call (using their hands-free device, of course). In serendipitous moments, someone who needs your product or service will see your information and use it and It cannot hurt to try. Girlfridayz can create magnets or decals for just a few pounds. In no time, you will be driving along with major marketing mojo.

Offer free consultations.

There are people in your community who want your advice. Give it to them for free.

Solid advice is hard to come by, especially if it is offered at no cost. Take the knowledge or experience that you have gained and give it to those who need it.

No obligation, no cost, and no-sales-pitch consulting sessions could be the best thing that ever happened to your business.

Some businesses offer workshops as a form of consultation. Instead of one-on-one sessions, they provide a free talk in their area of expertise — office wellness, children's nutrition, investment strategies, home-improvement ideas, etc. It does not hurt to offer free coffee and biscuits.

Host a meetup.

Local meetups are growing in popularity. Many of us are discovering that Facebook is a weak substitute for real face-to-face conversations.

Try hosting a meetup in your community. Select a relevant topic, pick a pleasant forum, and spread the word. It is a straightforward way to generate social buzz and make your business a community connector.

Remember, your marketing does not start with tactics. Marketing, regardless of its form, starts with a deep understanding of two things: 1) your business goals, and 2) your target customer.

Once you have these two things firmly in mind, it is time to unleash the marketing beast and lap up all leads you can and convert them into paying customers.

Just give stuff away at farmer's markets, trade shows, community events, on your website or on your storefront.

Written by Trisha Amable – Girlfridayz – Website: https://girlfridayz.com
Girllfridayz number 10358020 girlfriday, girlfridayz^{tm} is a registered trademark in the UK

Community involvement

Attend job fairs, and local political events, what about your local community? Are there ways to be involved in clubs, civic organisations, small local government positions, or the like?

Your community has all your prospects and customers because people form a community, and your neighbour can become your customers in an instant. Therefore, your local community is a very good source to advertise your business for the local people in your vicinity who might need your products or services. Your community can be your best ambassador when it regards your product or services if you live in a small village, you could become the go-to person who provides goods to the farmer community.

Being part of the community is a wonderful thing as you get to know people and strike up a conversation with them face to face, and this might lead to selling your product or services soon. As an example, I am very much involved in my community, I talked to the neighbouring companies' owners for years and as a result of it I got three companies who use my business regularly for various services and individual too mainly for computer maintenance but it still a sale. I was told that my approach was good, and I am friendly, so people are drawn to me. In my local co-op I speak to the staff and manager all the time we laugh and joke and banter together there is a staff who calls me trouble and I call him trouble for a joke, but because of my friendliness I can put my advertising material in the co-op and since I am allowed to do that, I got a few local customers. I also visit neighbouring areas to widen my scope and talk on occasions to random strangers, or people talking to me, and I end up giving my business card and speak briefly about what I do for a living and request politely to view my website and then go about my business. I also give a giveaway to my community every November a functional pen and Leather Pocket Diary, they love it so much that some people expect it.

A Persuasive tool

The headline "a persuasive tool" is alluring in its nature because it makes you think, and your imagination can run wild in summation of what it could be. Maybe it is a blunt or sharp tool or a sexy picture of a woman or a man without any clothes just there for imaginative thought about how to fix any issues or to be used for medical purposes to show an area needing to be mended. It could be a solution-oriented tool that provides useful data for the scientist to come up with a solution to a problem. It could be Sophia without her belly, and you see her motherboard may be enticing people to go into robotics. Whatever this tool is used for it deserved this headline A Persuasive tool. Have you guessed which tool it is yet?

Written by Trisha Amable – Girlfridayz – Website: https://girlfridayz.com
Girllfridayz number 10358020 girlfriday, girlfridayz[tm] is a registered trademark in the UK

What the above picture evokes in your mind? Pictures are very subjective and enticed the viewer to act on the information they provide, and they should be part of your arsenal when advertising your small business, but not always necessary as your content if interesting and valuable would not need a picture to support it.

Having said that a picture is necessary because it provides information to a cross-section of people who either have reading difficulties or do not like reading but need the information to access your business. Therefore, your picture should be informative and relevant to the written content about your business.

Using a picture alone to convey information about your business depending on its content can leave your viewer's mind to interpret and bring unexpected results as perception is a strong decisive point in people's decision-making. Therefore, using this marketing strategy combined with the Core Assets of marketing can result in a positive or negative outcome for your small business and should be used with good intention and a thoughtful process.

A picture alone can be used to create a marketing buzz which can affect the population of your country if your business is a well-known brand and loved by people. Here is an example of an excellent marketing buzz using just a picture and supportive text which made the UK talk sending some people into sheer panic, starting conspiracy theories about the business and starting panic buying mode about their beloved chicken.

Have you guessed which company I am talking about yet? Well, if you have not here is the picture which caused mayhem in the UK but resulted in an instant increase in revenue for the company.

But before you see this brilliant marketing strategy all done using one picture and clever content to generate one of the biggest marketing buzzes in the UK as it got the UK talking about their business logistic issue and pressing for result and return of operation, let me introduce to you **Scarcity Strategies** which are one of the most powerful marketing strategies to use if you are very skilful, and knowledgeable about the market and your customers you

Written by Trisha Amable – Girlfridayz – Website: https://girlfridayz.com
Girllfridayz number 10358020 girlfriday, girlfridayz™ is a registered trademark in the UK

can pull these marketing strategies with cautions as it can backfire if not executed well into disastrous consequential events for your company.

Scarcity strategy on occasion based on fear marketing that works because consumers are genuinely afraid of missing out on something which they perceive as valuable or essential to their survival. Fear marketing is tactical and must be done skilfully otherwise it can blow up in your face. Fear marketing strategies will make consumers take actions that benefit your business when done correctly as it often gives the consumers a sense of exclusivity.

You can implement them in your ads, email subject line, and email body in your CTA, however, done badly and maliciously can position your brand unfavourably and spark a negative buzz marketing about your company which will be difficult to recover due to the wide circulation it will receive.

It is best to use loss aversion to subtly create fear, one of the best ways to walk a safe line while using fear in your marketing and take advantage of loss aversion because people prefer avoiding losses to acquiring equivalents gains as it is better not to lose £100 than to find or gain £100.

Have you guessed which company I am talking about which used a picture to make the nation panic buy due to no chicken delivery and give a heartfelt apology to their customers, partners and associate and said the logistics problem with their supplier will be sorted swiftly and it was too?

But in these few days, we saw panic buying because their customers fear that they will not have any more chicken. We heard of their store's temporary closure they started buying a lot of chicken causing the company to up their revenue quickly due to the power of fear marketing. The customers feared missing out on their favourite chicken takeaway and bought more than usual. The strategy used was a picture subjective enough and their logo letter was re-arranged to create sympathy for their problem. It has also sparked curiosity and questions as well as disbelief due to their notoriety. Below is the company that did that brilliant marketing buzz.

Another buzz marketing was done by the government due to the Coronavirus a new strain of virus that killed older people in their 80 and younger people with underlying illnesses died due to catching the virus. The effect of COVID19 was felt worldwide and the country (UK) went into a lockdown and quarantine that caused people to panic buying food and caused superstore shelves to be empty. The government for safety informed the nation to stay home and work from home. if their staff was affected so as not to catch the virus and if they catch it to stay home for 7 days or 14 days. Safety messages were broadcasted for people to stay safe during the virus pandemic, and stricter restrictions were put in place by the Government.

Several businesses and establishments under the umbrella of safety faced closure and severe restrictions were put in place. This unprecedented move amid rumours of temporary closures — schools closed, major national events cancelled, larger businesses furloughed and small businesses closed through the Coronavirus safety major due to fear of catching the deadly virus.

The virus news has affected several countries in the world and we only heard about the death toll all over the world and the number of people affected causing sheer panic worldwide in some people hearing this terrible news and causing social isolation and stress on the medical worker and health industry, however, sales of protective mask increase and end up being sold on eBay has some people tried to capitalised on the sheer disaster worldwide and the panic.

As I am writing this playbook the pandemic is still the latest subject talked about and a trending topic as we constantly hear about COVID19 and its negative effect on people's health. President and Prime Minister have publicised catching it and emphasised they stay in hospital and came out beating the virus. New development towards a vaccine for this new strain of virus is underway with various companies and universities claiming to have developed a vaccine but none has been offered to anyone yet and it is not confirmed.

As the second wave of COVID19 strikes humanity the UK entering a second lockdown and predicting that the death toll will be higher than the one in the spring of 2020. The radio ads about COVID19 and safety messages are relentless the same message over again with new laws every week implemented and penalties for breaking restrictive measures because some people no longer respected or cared about the virus, some did not believe in it and some strongly believe in it therefore varied consumers opinions were felt, seen, and heard. Invention emerges and a Swiss company developed the safe-write pen which has an antiviral active solution in the barrel of the pen this would never have been developed if the world over were not in a pandemic, hence the virus provided an opportune moment for some company to put their thinking cap to develop useful protection for consumers against the biggest foe of humanity.

You can see the power of fear marketing can make people's businesses either suffer or other profits. To counteract the effect of the negative press the government are broadcasting prevention advice for public safety about how to protect ourselves from viral infection. This is the current situation while I am writing this playbook.

Marketing can be used in two ways to get people to listen by broadcasting advert on the radio or TV to reach many people worldwide and broadcast your message about your business this distribution channel are very efficient for distribution of news items by people either be good or bad and get the nation to act depending on the importance of the information passed on.

As you cannot market yourself to everybody it is not possible therefore the Pareto principle applied also known as the 80/20 rule the law of the vital few or the principal factor state that for many events 80% of the effects come from 20% of the cause. Applying this in your business and your marketing can make you more productive and target the right audience for your business.

As 80% of your result comes from 20% of your input. This rule is the general rule and is applied to everything in life this is why there is this famous marketing saying you cannot market

Written by Trisha Amable – Girlfridayz – Website: https://girlfridayz.com
Girllfridayz number 10358020 girlfriday, girlfridayz[tm] is a registered trademark in the UK

yourself to everybody therefore segmentation marketing is a must and your need to direct your effort to the right audience in your marketplace for your business either locally, nationally, or worldwide.

Using pictures in your marketing campaign creates engagement and increases conversion rates. The consumers viewing the picture can associate their thought with its meaning and interpretation. A picture speaks thousands of words to the viewer and can arouse curiosity and saucy thoughts to create delightful hot cuisine dishes.

Therefore, a good medium to use with your marketing message and your picture preferably should be associated with your message conveyed. In writing, your message ensures it is not in your industry vernacular, but a written message accompanied by a picture describing the product or service.

Marketing content with images receives on average 40% more shares than messages without a supporting picture. Relevant pictures introduce your theme and add colour and vibrancy to your content. An article with a relevant image also attracts more readership than a boring but mighty interesting article with no picture. Because on occasion lengthy business texts are part of your system thinking in your business and are called your business processes along with the systemise strategies and tactics used in your business that become part of your marketing arsenals.

A picture can represent a system or an algorithm. These two types of picture representation have different names and are called data modelling. Designing your new logical model depends on the business you are running you might need to know how to design these data flow models. As an example, here's an inventory system representing the cycle of a product in a specific colour. This model can be used to retarget your customers with the relevant offer and will be part of your internal system.

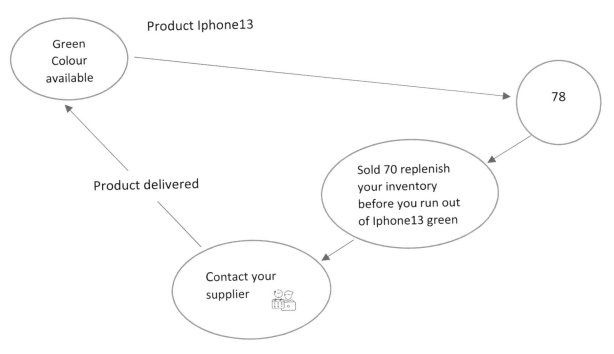

Written by Trisha Amable – Girlfridayz – Website: https://girlfridayz.com
Girllfridayz number 10358020 girlfriday, girlfridayz^tm is a registered trademark in the UK

SP

D

H

RW

CTA

WE'RE SORRY

A chicken restaurant without any chicken. It's not ideal. Huge apologies to our customers, especially those who travelled out of their way to find we were closed. And endless thanks to our KFC team members and our franchise partners for working tirelessly to improve the situation. It's been a hell of a week, but we're making progress, and every day more and more fresh chicken is being delivered to our restaurants. Thank you for bearing with us.

Visit kfc.co.uk/crossed-the-road for details about your local restaurant.

KFC in their marketing buzz is first using the marketing technique customer pain point. The key to marketing success is the customer's pain point. customers' pain point refers to the problems your customers face and how your product or service resolves those problems. In business, you should not think of customer pain points as something negative but rather as the reason that your business exists because once you start looking at your products or services from the viewpoint of your customers, everything you do, including marketing will be more targeted and effective.

KFC is also using the scarcity strategy combined with 6 Core Assets of marketing which are TM, H, RW, D, SP and a CTA. The content supporting the picture has all the mentioned tactics in it neatly tuck in but invisible and not that obvious to the reader in their heartfelt apology

Written by Trisha Amable – Girlfridayz – Website: https://girlfridayz.com
Girllfridayz number 10358020 girlfriday, girlfridayz^{tm} is a registered trademark in the UK

for their customers, teams, and franchise partners, drawing the reader into feeling their pain too creating sympathy for their business.

Pictures in marketing are a mighty tool to use as they provide invisible information to your viewer and stretch their imagination, therefore they should be used with caution and the information conveyed as its usefulness and value for the viewer to make an informed decision to purchase if accompanied with descriptive content to support the picture.

Bag it up with an exclusivity scarcity strategy

The Exclusive Scarcity strategy is a very useful and powerful strategy which involves skimming the marketplace in your industry by offering a high price for quality goods and the product or service; command its price.

This technique involves the distribution of a product or service on an unpredictable schedule and limited quantity, which creates artificial scarcity and exclusivity. This technique is mostly used with products, but it can be used with services as well.

Hermes Pink Leather Tote Bag reached up to £293,170 when a bag was sold at auction by Christie's for a record price in May 2017.

A bit of history about the Birkin Tote Bag the pictured Tote is a part of a line of tote bags by the French Luxury goods maker Hermes, that is handmade in leather and coined after Jane Birkin British actress and singer and was introduced in 1980. The bag experienced rapid growth and quickly became a symbol of wealth and exclusivity due to its high price and long waiting lists.

Birkin bags are Veblen goods and gives status and are the most popular bag amongst bag collectors in the world and was once seen as the rarest handbag in the world. The bag value as a matter of its intentionally high price has led it to be described as a Veblen good.

Hermes Boutique use an exclusivity scarcity strategy to market its tote product line to the wealthiest customers what attracts the chase after such a high price good is the rarity of it also the exquisite quality of the good and its simplicity in design. To create this elusive rarity in product distribution Hermes boutique keeps unpredictable schedules and limited quantities, which create what is called artificial scarcity and exclusivity.

The Exclusive Scarcity Strategy is the Queen of all marketing strategies as content is king. It is so powerful that on the back of it another strategy can be used by others that are accessing the upscale reseller second-hand marketplace. The bags have flooded the second-hand upscale market in no time and are frequently sold through this market and on social media.

And finally

The Core Assets combine with strategy work and it has been proven on many occasions you see the result daily with so many successful businesses and some are larger than others their success is because they are marketing themselves with the right technique and method and target their customer group but the real element of their success is the business processes that they have systemised which churning out sales by day, weeks, months and years as they constantly using them to sustain their business.

Remember there are only 9 tactics and 14 lead generations (9 tactics + 5 strategies) there is 13 conversion (9 tactics + 4 strategies) and there is 11 Multiplying customer value (9 tactics + 2 strategies) makes a total of 38 but it is 9 tactics plus 11 strategies to use in your marketing to acquire lead and conversion.

A Lead Magnet

Lead Magnet helps you acquire prospects therefore you can have several lead magnets. The Exclusive Member Club lead magnet is one of the best leads you can use. The Exclusive Member Club lead magnet comes with an attached referral template. Once you capture the potential customer details you can then offer a prize draw, competition or give a gift.

The latter leads convert prospects into customers effectively. You can use the cross-sell strategy after they purchase your product with a complimentary product or service offer. You can upsell your customer with two products of different quality and prices. You can down-sell with a discount. The latter can be for the member of your exclusive club only. With the exclusive lead magnet people, part of your exclusive club will talk to their peers about your exclusive club and entice new members to join because of the benefit the exclusive club offer.

You can apply the exclusive club lead on Facebook due to the group creation possibility and on your website too.

Another effective lead you can do is a Special Report, you are demonstrating your expertise in one subject. You can give it for free, but you asked for the name and email. You can ask for their address and explain why you are requiring an address; "We wish to send a gift on a special occasion", and you list the occasion. With the details gathered you can down-sell them to give the prospect an incentive to buy something associated with your free report. For example, we wrote a Special Report titled 26 Common Website Design Mistakes That Cripple Your Online Business and How to Avoid Them.

69

Written by Trisha Amable – Girlfridayz – Website: https://girlfridayz.com
Girllfridayz number 10358020 girlfriday, girlfridayz[tm] is a registered trademark in the UK

This is a fantastic lead magnet which can get you, customers. Because it allows you to convert your prospect into qualified paying customers. Also, the people reading your special report see you as an expert in your field. Demonstrating your expertise in your industry allows you to charge a higher fee for your expertise and you tend to get lucrative customers.

Sale letter

Another effective lead magnet can double up as conversion straight off the bat when you push just one product at a time especially if your sale letter is a small order form and a sample of your product is enclosed or a picture of the product. And this same sale letter with an order form can be reused. You can send it to your existing customer with another offer related to their previous purchase and there you go a perfect system. You acquire leads and then convert them into paying customers then you can cross-sell with another product or an offer or an upsell and then build a business system as you can switch the strategies used depending on the context.

Direct Sale Pitch – Natural conversation

A face-to-face meeting with people is the best to acquire leads, sales, and contact. You cannot beat direct contact which is not pitching your business at all but a genuine conversation with people without trying to sell them anything at all.

They will naturally tell you what they do for a living and if your approach is right, you will get so much insight into the person you speaking to because you are exchanging information about each other without stressing and you will be amazed at how much a person can give you about them without you even asking.

With the information gathered you can get their details to further your conversation and offer your products or services as a solution if you sense the problem they may have, and you come as the solution.

This method required considerable skills. Conversational skills require a good approach meaning friendly but professional and you are willing to disclose about yourself too to ensure that the exchange remains friendly because you be amazed at what you can achieve when you pay a genuine interest in people. You need to be naturally extroverted and genuinely like people. if you are this type of person, you will achieve the most sales ever and acquire the most lead, contact and business awareness. Here is an example below.

The benefit of promoting your business face to face

On LinkedIn, I posted this in my feed about three days ago about what is a direct sales pitch – a natural conversation.

In London, the weather was fantastic 30 degrees, amazing for London everyone was at the park with family.

70

Written by Trisha Amable – Girlfridayz – Website: https://girlfridayz.com
Girllfridayz number 10358020 girlfriday, girlfridayz^{tm} is a registered trademark in the UK

We decided to join the crowd at girlfridayz and took with us our brochures and our business card. It was such a productive day just spoke to 9 strangers by approaching people and got two solid referrals and two people who will contact me to use our business.

The last person we spoke to for two hours solid ended up doing exercises together and showed her the way to the station. I give her exercise tips and she viewed my website on the spot using my iPhone. She discussed my services offer and like our online store and business tools calculators that she used and viewed our artwork and design page. She said she'll look at the remaining of our website when she gets home.

I impressed some people and I even manage to get them to view our award video and took 4 brochures, plus 6 business cards for friends and got a bicycle ride offer for our next consultation brilliant productive day for us at Girlfridayz.

You see using social media has its benefit, but you cannot beat real conversations with people. Here is how this conversation started — The last person I spoke to share the same interest in riding a bicycle with me. I started the conversation by discussing bicycles next that got the conversation started and I secured a customer plus referrals.

Analysis of my day using direct sales pitch – natural conversation.

I have an extrovert personality meaning an outgoing, socially confident person; hence it is easy for me to achieve this unassuming strategy and use it in my business to acquire leads, referrals, and customers. This works as a treat if used with approachable and observational skills. You begin to notice behaviours and body language; you can use these observations to your advantage by adapting your mannerism.

In the back of my post, I got a new connection who loves my post so much and decided to offer me an interview.

Here's our exchange

AH: "I'm working on a new series and am interviewing digital experts in their respective fields. It gives me great content to share with my tribe and is good personal branding for my guests. Would you be open to being interviewed?"

Me: My topic is my Marketing Playbook: The Core Assets of Marketing Revealed

AH: "What would you cover within that, just so I know the kind of questions to ask? Also, when can we hop on Zoom for the interview?"

Me: give me the time my email is girlfridayz@girlfidayz.com

AH: "2 pm tomorrow ok?"

Me: Sure

Written by Trisha Amable – Girlfridayz – Website: https://girlfridayz.com
Girllfridayz number 10358020 girlfriday, girlfridayz[tm] is a registered trademark in the UK

The interview took place on 26/06/20 and he allowed me to promote this Marketing Playbook it was a very insightful interview because at some point I asked him how he gets high-paying clients he replied just like me and does not speak to people who cannot commit to £5000 budget for his services as it does not entertain people with £100 to £200 budget and added now you are interviewing me which I replied an interview is a two ways process and he replied yes it is.

Because he said this, I perceived that he was someone who value content and I offered him to read inside our Marketing Playbook or to purchase it directly. I sensed that he has an appreciation for quality content and quality good therefore a good person to appreciate the wealth of information this playbook provides you with. (Gentle Persuasion)

I was right because he liked our interview so much. I made him feel comfortable and he invited me to his YouTube Channel and Facebook Group also he said he will add a link to my online store for others to purchase my playbook.

He said that I provided so much valuable information about my playbook and valuable content for business growth for small businesses that it is the content which is valuable, and he will share this interview across his network. (On the spot Feedback SP)

The interview terminated see below what he said and share on LinkedIn including LinkedIn pages many people participate in this # topic which is called referrals.

"I had the pleasure of speaking to Trisha Amable,(referral) an award-winning entrepreneur who is also the CEO of Girlfridayz. (H)

Normally I interview someone who is branded as a 'mini-guru' so it was quite good to catch up with a consultant who is more down-to-Earth (RW)

We spoke about how small businesses are not using social media correctly and also the various marketing playbooks she has written, you can grab them here: (CTA)

https://lnkd.in/dSR85UV (CTA)

If you are running a digital or social media marketing business, join our free community on Facebook, where we discuss how to grow your agency by getting high-ticket clients: (cross sales but missing text to link the CTA link to entice people to click on the link he could have said access our group via the link below more specific)

https://lnkd.in/dD7Ykq3 (CTA)

#smallbusinessmarketing #agency #socialmediamarketing #digitalmarketing #smma #marke tingagency #marketingconsultant #socialmedia #smallbusinesses " (Referrals)

You can see the power of direct sales pitch – natural conversation and the benefits it brings to your business instantly, therefore muster the courage to speak to a total stranger and start

Written by Trisha Amable – Girlfridayz – Website: https://girlfridayz.com
Girllfridayz number 10358020 girlfriday, girlfridayz^tm is a registered trademark in the UK

a conversation with them without trying to sell your product or services as the opportunity to speak about your product or services will come soon enough during this innocent conversation and if you come prepared as we did with our brochure and business card just in case we spark interest and people ask you do have a business card or you can offer your business card and brochure straight of the bat.

We even managed to give our mobile phone with our website page open and let the last person we spoke to happily scrolled to the pages which interested her still conversing and she used our business calculators, view our online store including playbook, design and printing page and said she would refer some of her clients to us when it is too much for her for website design and asked if I could do the design requested I say yes plus she added her contact details in my phone.

You see the power of a direct sales pitch – natural conversation with people this strategy works like a treat. Pay a genuine interest in people and you can gain so much for your business.

This strategy is not to be confused with manipulative personality which is different as manipulative is more deceitful it is to control or influence a person or situation cleverly or unscrupulously therefore exploiting. It is a valid strategy to use but not recommended as you set your business as deceitful and when found out you lose a lot of customers.

Print Marketing

Print marketing refers to your business information printed on varied items such as your wall banners or imprinted on pens or cups etc. It is the king of all marketing strategies and can beat online marketing which copies all print marketing and brought them online, however, the value and benefit print marketing bring cannot be ignored as it brings your business awareness to passerby and possible prospects, keep your customers top of mind because if they have your keyring, or drink a cup of coffee in your mug with your business details on it they are more likely to remember you.

If you have a business event online or in a hall or conference your rolling banner is your best friend as it displays all your business information in a big font and people attending the event cannot miss it. Your flyers and business card plus a three-fold brochure can be given on the spot to anybody when you use a direct pitch strategy like we did when we went to the park on that sunny day.

I cannot stress enough the value of king marketing (print marketing) because you can give away a present to your customers with your business on it or send a sample of your product to potential customers or new customers to keep them buying from you.

As an example, we give our local community a leather pocket duo Windsor diary and a functional pen every November they love it. They have our website domain name and phone number on it with the following message compliment of Girlfridayz Limited. Hence make print

Written by Trisha Amable – Girlfridayz – Website: https://girlfridayz.com
Girllfridayz number 10358020 girlfriday, girlfridayz[tm] is a registered trademark in the UK

marketing part of your arsenal to increase interest in your business, and acquire prospects and customers.

Distribution Marketing

The process of making your product or service available for the consumers or business user who needs it is called distribution which is part of the marketing mix 4ps or you can refer to it as place. Decisions about your distribution need to be taken in line with your company vision and overall strategic planning for better results and achieving ROI (Return on Investment).

Social Post an Omnichannel Strategic Move

Social Post, Tweet, Video, Picture, Messenger, Bots, Pins, Stories, Chat, WhatsApp etc are effective lead magnets when used with the 9 tactics and all lead magnets are most effectively used with the 9 tactics or 8 if you do not have social proof anything less than 8 or 9 tactics your result will be poor. I am not saying that you are not getting customer but not a massive amount and your business remain macro or small.

The social media platform types of content display are considered Digital Marketing and it's called omnichannel distribution marketing because omnichannel is a cross-channel content strategy that you can use to improve your user experience and drive better relationships with your audience across a point of contact.

Omnichannel implies integration and orchestration of channels such that the experience of engagement across all channels provides a better user experience and product or service exposure for users of these platforms and can generate engagement and sales through one medium or the other as well as enquiry or visit to your brick and mortar or website. Omnichannel distribution has proven itself to be more efficient and pleasant than the use of a single channel in isolation.

Omnichannel supersedes multichannel and includes channels such as physical locations and environments, eCommerce, mobile applications, social media and emerging formats like augmented mixed reality or dynamically personalised video.

Using omnichannel in your business contends that a customer values the ability to engage with you through multiple avenues at the same time should you use your business on multiple platforms to promote your services or products. However, it is important to note that it is practically impossible for most businesses to use all channels at once. Therefore, an omnichannel strategy needs to support only the channel that you can manage and provide true engagement.

What Omnichannel Look Like

Here is an example to show you what an omnichannel distribution strategy looks like we are using the company Mission Workshop, a leader in the weatherproof bag and technical apparel space, and your prospective customer can expect something like the following omnichannel retargeting sequence:

Day 1

The focus is on the high-level benefits of the duffle bag, The Cadre 26.

Figure 4 image from Mission Workshop

Before viewing the ad, the prospect may not have known the name of the duffel bag he or she recently viewed. The prospect may have seen the price tag of £184 and abandoned the site without making themselves aware of the description highlighting the feature and benefits of the bag its durability and its lifetime guarantee offer.

Later, as the prospect browses Instagram on his or her phone, he or she sees this image which is more focused on the lifestyle behind the brand.

Day 1 retargeting exposes the prospect to more information about the brand and products throughout multiple touchpoints without forcing the prospect to visit the website again. The ads aim to educate instead of pressure the prospect to make a purchase.

Day 2 The messaging evolves and exposes the prospect to new media formats, layers, and brand offerings. The retargeting sequence might include a video of the bag in action while the shopper is on Facebook.

It might be followed by a pre-roll ad for a product review while the prospect is browsing YouTube bag reviews.

Day 3 Rather than exclusively promoting the higher-priced bag, the brand might use Facebook's Product Collection Unit to highlight the other product categories they sell. In effect using the cross-sell strategy is showing your other related product or services which may be priced at a lower value or as an offer on price.

While browsing the web, the prospect might see retargeting ads featuring the same products found in the featured collection area on Google's marketplace. This creates consistency across channels and familiarizes the prospect with the brand's offerings.

Day 4 The prospect may see Facebook advertising prompting him or her to visit a local retail partner or offer a free consultation with a stylist.

Following the consultation with the stylist, the prospect makes a purchase. The stylist follows up with an email inviting the customer to an upcoming Mission Workshop trunk show. To attend the show, the customer must create an account to register on the business site.

By registering to their website, a customer's profile is entered into the company's CRM and segmented for future marketing. Over four days and eight touchpoints, Mission Workshop executes an omnichannel strategy that educates the shopper on:

77

Written by Trisha Amable – Girlfridayz – Website: https://girlfridayz.com
Girllfridayz number 10358020 girlfriday, girlfridayz^{tm} is a registered trademark in the UK

1. The product mix.
2. The guarantee
3. The review
4. Where to engage with the brand in person

The messaging is channel-relevant, moves the prospect down the sale funnel, and converts the prospect into a customer by bridging the digital and physical worlds.

Can you see how useful is omnichannel you can turn the users of these platforms into your customers and move the user down your sale funnel and provide a brand experience which leads to a purchase and the user becoming a loyal customer.

Multichannel Marketing is a Brilliant Strategy

Multichannel marketing is the blending of different distribution and promotional channels for Marketing. Distribution channels range from a retail storefront, a website, or a mail order catalogue and brochures.

Multichannel marketing is more about choice and its objective is to make it easier for a consumer to purchase a company product or service in whatever is most appropriate. The effectiveness of multichannel marketing is obtained by having good, supported supply chain management systems in place, so the details and prices of goods on offer are consistent across the different channels.

It might also be supported by a detailed analysis of the return on investment from each different channel, measured in terms of customer response and conversion of sales. The contribution each channel delivers to sales can be assessed via marketing mix modelling or attribution modelling.

The marketing mix modelling refers to statistical analysis such as multivariate regression on sales and marketing time series data to estimate the impact of various marketing tactics (marketing mix) on sales and then forecast the impact of future sales sets of tactics and is often used to optimised advertising mix and promotional tactics concerning sales revenue or profit.

Attribution Marketing refers to the identification of a set of user actions ("events" or "touchpoints") that contribute to the desired outcome, and then the assignment of a value to each of these events. Marketing Attribution provides a level of understanding of what combination of events in what order influences individuals to engage in the desired behaviour, typically referred to as a conversion.

Some companies target certain channels at different demographic segments of the market or different socio-economic groups of consumers. Multichannel Marketing allows the retail merchant to reach its prospective or current customer in a channel of his or her liking.

While multichannel marketing mainly focuses primarily on new media platforms in marketing, traditional approaches use old media such as print marketing, telemarketing, direct mail, and

78

Written by Trisha Amable – Girlfridayz – Website: https://girlfridayz.com
Girllfridayz number 10358020 girlfriday, girlfridayz[tm] is a registered trademark in the UK

broadcasting stations such as radio and television as well as podcasting. Multichannel Marketing does not only use web 2.0 forms but also integrates customer interaction through various platforms such as via text messaging, on a website, email, online video campaigns, and GPS to track the location of a customer and their proximity to the product or service. Being able to reach out to customers directly is an important marketing strategy because it is convenient and enhances direct customer interaction.

There are Enormous Benefits in Using Multichannel

Some of the long-term benefits of this style of Marketing include:

- ✓ Better management of results and sales when using many communicative platforms to reach your audience increases the chances of receiving feedback from a variety of customers' overall performances. This feedback gives your company an idea of what your customers want and what you can improve upon.

- ✓ Higher revenues as the more diverse platforms are used in trying to reach your customers, the more your potential customers are likely to reach out to purchase your goods or services. If you only advertise your brand on the internet, it will be very hard for you to capture the attention of customers who do not use the internet regularly and rely on other mediums such as television or radio or printed materials for example.

- ✓ You get a better understanding of your customers through your customers' responses, and it is easier for you to understand what they expect from your product or service, and you see how your brand could be improved to satisfy the needs of your customer. To create a niche, it is necessary to identify the channels and platforms which work for a certain group of customers for example pet lovers or coffee lovers' groups will be targeted with relevant ads about those groups.

- ✓ You can increase your brand visibility and reach because about 36% of buyers search for products on one channel but purchase the product through a different channel.

- ✓ You increase business awareness and enquiry about your business.

A Coordinated Effort

Companies that sell branded products and services through local businesses market over both online and offline channels to local audiences. Online and offline multichannel marketing campaigns can either inform one another or are executed in isolation. A proportion of companies use their online marketing efforts to inform their offline advertising. The following strategy is used: they test keywords online to understand if they fit with customer intent before printing them in offline ads.

Flyers, catalogue, newspaper ad if you used the bigger size offer or even in the small size you can fit 3 to 5 tactics or 9 depending on the medium used.

Your website is the biggest lead magnet if you use the 9 tactics in your website content coupled with the strategies you've gone clear. If you do not believe look at Amazon, the best online website, and the richest e-commerce business. Do you want to know why we say this at Girlfridayz, it is because they are using the Core Assets of marketing all over their website and the 11 strategies on every page, they are huge on the social proof component all the tactics are visible in everything they do their processes are well oil and systemised and they pulling customer by the million worldwide?

Pest bothers me not when success is within my reach.

A PESTEL analysis is important for business continuity, let define what is a PESTEL analysis and then why as a business you need to conduct one. A PESTEL is a framework a tool used by all good marketers to analyze and monitor the macro-environment (external marketing environment) factors that have an impact on an organisation. The result of this is used to identify threats and weaknesses which is used in a SWOT analysis.

PESTEL stand for Political, Economic, Social, Technology, Environmental and Legal. We are going to look a bit more into each criterion and why it's important to conduct a PESTEL analysis before conducting a SWOT analysis for your business.

It is very useful to conduct A PESTEL analysis before starting up your own business for your existing business, as it would give you a strong indication of the impact the criterion has on your business depending on the industry you decide that you want to start up a business or currently operating if you would require any legal or political standard that you will need to abide by and other important factors which can affect your start-up or your business.

Let's delve into each criterion.

Political Factors: These are all about how and to what degree a government intervenes in the economy. This can include – government policy, political stability or instability in overseas markets, foreign trade policy, tax policy, labour law, environmental law, trade restrictions and so on.

Political factors often have an impact on a business and how they do business. Businesses need to be able to respond to the current and anticipated future legislation and adjust their marketing policy accordingly. *(Example of this Brexit, the coronavirus Pandemic worldwide, and The war between Russia and Ukraine.)*

Economic Factors: Economic factors have a significant impact on how an organisation does business and how profitable they are. Factors include – economic growth, interest rates, exchange rates, inflation, disposable income of consumers and businesses and so on.

Written by Trisha Amable – Girlfridayz – Website: https://girlfridayz.com
Girllfridayz number 10358020 girlfriday, girlfridayz^{tm} is a registered trademark in the UK

These factors can be further broken down into macroeconomic and microeconomic factors. Macroeconomic factors deal with the management of demand in any given economy. Governments use interest rate control, taxation policy and government expenditure as the main mechanisms they use for these Micro-economic factors are all about the way people spend their incomes. This has a large impact on B2C organisations.

Social Factors: Also known as Socio-Cultural factors are the areas that involve the shared belief and attitudes of the population. These factors include – population growth, age distribution, health consciousness, career attitudes and so on. And you also include Social Media movement and belief, plus social technology advancement and innovation.
These factors are of interest as they have a direct effect on how marketers understand customers and what drives them.

Technological Factors: We all know that we entered **the digital age** and how fast technology changes the face of business and how this impacts the way we market our products or services. With the boom of Social Media platforms, app development, and mobile phone used for business deals these days it is a commodity and a way of conducting business nowadays.

Technological factors affect marketing and the management thereof in three distinct ways:

1. New ways of producing goods and services
2. New ways of distributing goods and services
3. New ways of communicating with target markets

Environmental Factors: These factors have only really come to the forefront in the last fifteen years or so. They have become important due to the increasing scarcity of raw materials, pollution targets, doing business as an ethical and sustainable company, and carbon footprint targets set by governments *(this is a good example where one factor could be classed as political and environmental at the same time)*.
These are just some of the issues marketers are facing within this factor. More and more consumers are demanding that the products they buy are sourced ethically, and if possible, from a sustainable source.

Legal Factors: Legal factors include - health and safety, equal opportunities, advertising standards, consumer rights and laws, product labelling and product safety.

Companies need to know what is and what is not legal to trade successfully. If an organisation trades globally this becomes a very tricky area to get right as each country has its own set of rules and regulations. So, it is best to conduct market research so to speak doing your homework to ensure that you are not breaking any laws before starting your own business or conducting your business.

PESTEL analysis is the greatest tool you need to use in your business it helps you to understand where your business can operate and how to see where you can make your mark by abiding by the rules and other people affecting your business. It is important as it helps understand and adjust your business according to your finding. Without a plan you are planning to fail

Written by Trisha Amable – Girlfridayz – Website: https://girlfridayz.com
Girllfridayz number 10358020 girlfriday, girlfridayz^{tm} is a registered trademark in the UK

therefore planning is mighty important for business success and business goals setting, objectives, vision and ultimately action on your plan is needed to achieve success.

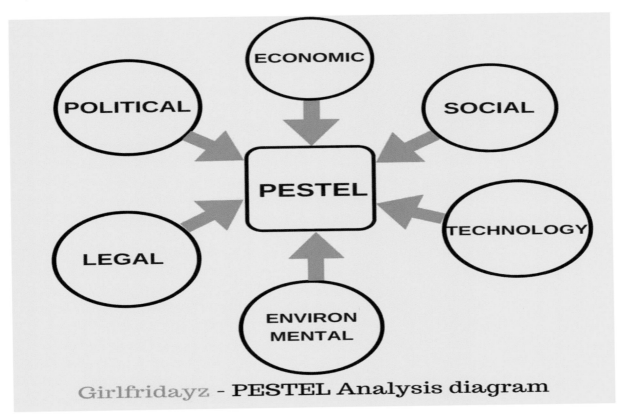

Girlfridayz - **PESTEL Analysis diagram**

The latter are the explanation of each criterion; hence you can see that a PESTEL analysis is a very useful tool to determine the steps you must take to conduct business in your chosen industry to remain legal and ensure that your company can be sustainable in the current economic climate, the technology involves for your business sustainability or product developments, consumers and government influences, plus environmental climate can make or break your business.

It is important to look at all these factors which can either affect or benefit your business once you conducted a thorough in-depth PESTEL analysis you can then proceed to conduct a SWOT analysis as it is important to incorporate a SWOT analysis within your PESTEL and if you are a conscientious business and care about the processes of your business the importance of PEST analysis in strategic management and marketing strategy becomes relevant to your overall growth strategy.

A PESTEL including a SWOT analysis should be part of your **business plan** and also a base for your **content strategy**.

82

Written by Trisha Amable – Girlfridayz – Website: https://girlfridayz.com
Girllfridayz number 10358020 girlfriday, girlfridayz[tm] is a registered trademark in the UK

International SWOT Analysis for Brick and Mortar Businesses

Strengths	Weaknesses
• Infrastructure in place • Volunteers • Strong Economy • Good Political standing	• Lack of infrastructure • The size of the country • uncertain political and economic stability
Opportunity • Growth in your industry • Business development • Quality of life increase • Use of post-event legacy • Development of infrastructure	**Threats** • The cost • Pollution • Reliance on your industry rejuvenating the economy • Displacement of residents

Girlfridayz

Marshmallow me with a Maslow's Pyramid

Customers are the belly of any business without food and water you have very little chance of surviving so is your business without customers, therefore, knowing what your customers need you can provide a solution to their needs, and they will pay you for your valuable, useful services or products provided.

Maslow's hierarchy in your Marketing is very good. Maslow is the creator of the Maslow hierarchy a specialist in human behavioural psychology. The hierarchy was first developed to help explain the connection between basic human needs and human desires.

In businesses, organisations, families, or home businesses the descriptive traits of human beings can portray in a lifetime are your customers and vice versa you could be their customers. You always asked yourself what people want when running a business and try to please your customers or potential customers. Without relating to or understanding your customer's behaviour traits you would be able to provide a solution to their needs. Only when you grasp Maslow's hierarchy of needs you will be able to understand people and their needs, therefore, more likely to achieve a successful sale.

Written by Trisha Amable – Girlfridayz – Website: https://girlfridayz.com
Girllfridayz number 10358020 girlfriday, girlfridayz[tm] is a registered trademark in the UK

- For everybody, valuable commodities represent a lifetime value only when someone is willing to trade a portion of his or her lifetime for them.
- Each of us depends on our upbringing and environment this increase in value may shape our mindset and attention to what we want the most in life.
- To some it all doom and gloom, scepticism, deep-seated fear, and doubt or to be like or worthy of anything or worrying been made fun of and worry about the slightest thing needing reassurance that they are just fine and will sail through life unscaled.
- To most, it is fame and glory and leaving their mark in history or touching the world with wisdom.
- For many people, it is the freedom of monetary wealth, because time is not money by itself, but it is your life that has value and the people who spend their lifetime providing value to other gains monetary wealth. (Trisha Amable)
- For others, they seek approval and respect for professional success, achieving successful sales in their business and filling up their database with customers to ensure constant success the high number and popularity is their driver.
- To others the desirability of their sexual partners and the well-being of their offspring, family, and friends, and to some the sacrifice of their time for the benefit of those in need.

Since we moved into the digital world for businesses new concept based on older concepts has been created cyberpsychology colloquially known as digital psychology encompasses all psychology field phenomena relating to emerging technology and the human mind and behaviour and how technology culture has changed perspective but has not changed human needs.

Therefore a social media presence is imperative to keep your business relevant and moving forward for customers acquisition as brick and mortar businesses enjoy both medium communities presence and an online presence as we now have online communities therefore the customers' acquisition is not widened but move online henceforward it makes sense to follow the movement but also to access your local shop and businesses as earth community is needed for the survival of the human race as we need each other to grow and our survival depends on it.

Maslow's Pyramid of needs is very relevant to customers acquisition and based on his finding you can influence your sales to the right people for your target market using various marketing strategies combined with the tactics such as fear marketing for this group of people the one with a deep-seated fear and worry, therefore, scarcity strategy work and you come with the solution, you need to talk money with the money orientated people who after fame and glory they will respond favourably to the skimming strategy and exclusive scarcity. For popularity lovers and higher the number, you need to arouse their vanity with number strategies such 10000 bought it you miss out if your not part of it.

For the frugal people you need to offer irresistible discount prices they will lap it up and with sceptical people, you talk fact and may be science on how what you provide is good and show social proof every group respond to psychology we are designed this way and you need to show the benefit of using your product or services people respond more to benefit than feature the feature support the benefit of using your product or service.

It introduces your products or services, but it is how this feature will be beneficial that matters most to customers. Conduct a customer behaviour persona to achieve sales with the right group of people according to your target market. Customer's behaviour persona looks at demographic, income bracket, interest, education and country bases, culture, religion, belief as all these can affect sales so knowing how to navigate with customers and providing a solution to their need one need to do one.

How to define your target market

We going to demonstrate to you how to build a customer's Avatar in effect what we called a customer behaviour persona. In building your Avatar you will need to identify your customers and then build the Avatar. I.e.: if your business support B2B (business to business) customers you will need to find what type of business they are running if it is products or services and if they spend money on their marketing as well as other variables.

You need to look at these criteria Demography, Psychography, Paint Point, Common Objection, and individualism.

Demography: What size is the business, number of employees, age of the business, turnover, location, number of directors, industry type any other variables?

Psychographics (segmentation): What motivates decision-makers in the business to act, behaviours, values, hobbies, and the impact of decisions for businesses and for people who are running the business. The segmentation process will be different for everyone.

Paint Points: What they want most and need, what is most efficient, ease of use of the solution provided, time and anything else.

Common Objection: There most common reason not to buy or not the exact cost of the product or services or time wasted.

Individualism: Service or product expertise.

By doing the latter you get a holistic view of your target market, and you are more likely to target the right audience for your services and products. The term psychographics is a fancy term for segmentation meaning that you need to segment your market. Simply because you cannot market yourself to everyone and everyone will not be interested in what you are selling. You can determine your niche to be local, national, or international but you need to take into consideration your customer Avatar which helps you to define the right audience for yourself.

Written by Trisha Amable – Girlfridayz – Website: https://girlfridayz.com
Girllfridayz number 10358020 girlfriday, girlfridayz[tm] is a registered trademark in the UK

See how we targeted on social media the CPA Accountant Sole practitioner with up to 4 partners using an Avatar.

Segmentation practical example based on our post on LinkedIn and Facebook.

Are you an accountant CPA accredited sole practitioner with up to 4 partners? (H)(TM)

We have a solution to the problem you are facing right now which is maximising your existing customers' value and relieving your worry about accounting software that you may feel replacing your job at a click of a few buttons. (Paint Point Strategy used)

Our solution is simple and very effective. It is a simple alternative(D)(RW) if you are willing to try to increase your clients and close the deal at the right fee for your expertise and gain a competitive advantage over your competitor.

If this sounds like a solution that you can try to maximise your customer's value, we at Girlfridayz Limited can support you to change your existing marketing to increase your business profitability with our scalable blend of services result orientated through a cognitive approach solution benefiting your accountancy practice.

Visit https://girlfridayz.com/it-all-about-you to access our blend of services and result-orientated approach to benefit your accountancy practice. (CTA)

#accountantcy #accountant #CPAaccountant (referral)

In this post that I put on my social media platforms, you can see that I am targeting the right audience for my services and a specific audience too as we provide support to B2B mainly SMEs therefore this post was targeted to our client group and specific industry. We were able to do this by first building an Avatar about the CPA account and researching the variable needed then deciding to use the paint point strategy. We used 5 tactics and 1 strategy which is effective aim to use at least 5 to 9 tactics with one strategy for maximum return.

Manifesting financial abundance in your business

Money is the fundamental necessity of life. Money exerts more power over us than any other single commodity. Money rules our lives.

Manifesting financial abundance is the number one reason most people learn about the law of attraction techniques. While the manifestation tools can be successfully used to attract financial success, obtaining abundance needs dedication, hard work, patience, and persistence.

The universe will start to support your financial dreams when you believe in yourself, become persistent and look for ways to tackle your ambitious goals. When you become obsessed with your goals and do what is necessary.

The journey of financial abundance starts from within. Wealth is a state of mind, and when you learn how to attain that state of mind, your life will change forever.

Do you know that your attitude toward money is the biggest barrier that keeps you from attaining financial freedom? What separates rich from poor is not just the amount of money they possess, financially successful people tend to think differently. So how to develop the thinking pattern that attracts riches? We'll learn it as we move along.

Setting Your "Financial Thermostat"

Setting up your financial thermostat is the very first thing you should do if you want to attain financial abundance. Many hardworking people fail to do well in life because they live with a financial thermostat setting that they have inherited from their upbringing.

It may seem hard to believe, but according to research, 70 per cent of people who win a lottery end up returning to their original financial state, regardless of the size of their winning.

You'll only have the amount of money you can comfortably handle. If your financial "thermostat" is set for thousands, no matter how many millions you own by accident, you'll end up having thousands.

Ask yourself how much money you need to live your dream. If it requires even 1000x as much money as you have now (or more), don't worry. Set your financial thermostat for that amount. Whenever you experience a negative thought like, **"you don't deserve that"**. Challenge that

thought and say, *"Of course I do!"* You must keep enforcing the positive thoughts to break through your limiting money beliefs.

Building a Healthy Relationship with Money

People, who don't maintain a healthy relationship with money hardly have a consistent money strategy. They often spend more than they earn. They view money with fear and frustration instead of treating money like a trusted friend.

This kind of mindset can only lead to an impoverishment of life. Because when you have an unhealthy relationship with money, you will focus your attention on scarcity, rather than abundance. And according to the law of attraction, if you rest your focus on scarcity, you'll attract only scarcity.

To change your relationship with money, spend some time understanding your money behaviour and your financial self-image.

Forgive yourself for all the money mistakes you made in the past. We all made bad money decisions in the past. If we fail to forgive ourselves, it will be hard for us to make real progress. Let go of your past mistakes and embrace your current financial situation.

Face your money fears. Set aside one hour every week to review your checking and savings accounts and credit card balances.

Written by Trisha Amable – Girlfridayz – Website: https://girlfridayz.com
Girllfridayz number 10358020 girlfriday, girlfridayz[tm] is a registered trademark in the UK

Affirmations help to cultivate a positive money mindset. Use the following affirmations to improve your relationship with money:

- The universe is a constant supplier of money for me
- I love money and money loves me back
- I'm consciously happy and positive about money
- There are no limits to the amount of money I can possess
- My relationship with money is thriving.
- Developing Rich Habits

Almost half of our daily activities are habits, and these habits shape our lives far more than we probably realize. Habits can make your rich or poor or keep you stuck in the middle class. Habits are the basis of your success or downfall. To achieve financial abundance, you must adopt rich habits and drop poor habits.

Draw two columns on a piece of paper. Under column one, list your bad daily habits. Under column two list their opposite habits, which are going to be your new rich habits.

Here is an example:

Bad daily habits	Good daily habits
I don't exercise regularly	I will exercise for 30 minutes every day.
I go to bed late at night	I'll go to bed between 10 and 10:30 pm every night.
I always leave things to the last minute	I'll make sure to accomplish every task on my to-do list every day
I use my mobile phone before bedtime	I won't use my mobile phone before bedtime
I eat too many junk foods	I'll cut the junk food from my day and save it as a treat.

Wrap-Up: Bringing financial abundance into your life is not difficult when you're doing it one step at a time. However, shifting the mindset from scarcity to abundance needs some work. Reset your financial thermostat, improve your relationship with money, develop rich habits and continue to work on your vision— the universe will guide you toward your goal.

The Importance of using Maslow's Pyramid in your business is immense for customers and prospect acquisition because Maslow discusses our human basic needs. Hereto you will find a picture of Maslow's pyramid and an explanation of each criterion of the pyramid. You will notice its usefulness for your marketing and its application to your business when it comes to audience attraction.

Written by Trisha Amable – Girlfridayz – Website: https://girlfridayz.com
Girllfridayz number 10358020 girlfriday, girlfridayz^{tm} is a registered trademark in the UK

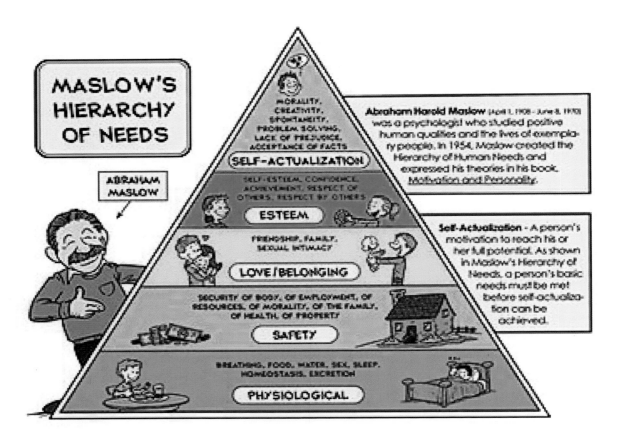

Maslow's pyramid contains 5 criteria which are described below:

Physiological needs:

These are the underlying needs we as humans cannot live without. E.g., Food, water, sleep, oxygen etc.

Safety needs:

We all need to feel safe. Whether that be physically, financially or job security and health.

Social needs:

We all look for social connections in friends and family.

Esteem needs:

We all desire to have respect and be respected by others, this includes self-esteem, confidence, and a sense of self-achievement.

Self-actualisation:

This is realising one's full potential, and this will differ from person to person. This is the highest level on the hierarchy and what we are all striving for.

If marketers know the wants and needs of their target market (which every good marketer should!) then this can be used as a selling point to influence sales if you actually combine the

89

Written by Trisha Amable – Girlfridayz – Website: https://girlfridayz.com
Girllfridayz number 10358020 girlfriday, girlfridayz[tm] is a registered trademark in the UK

two psychological model for maximum sales gain from consumers or innovate a product that answer the needs and wants of the consumers that will improve their life, or you have innovated some smart solution and find a way to offer a perceived value to the consumers to sell your products or services.

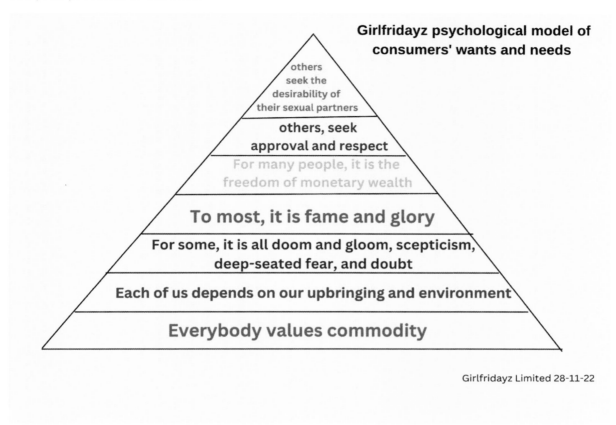

Use psychology marketing in your business to acquire customers and target your marketing to the right customer using the 7 criteria of our Girlfridayz psychological consumers' wants and needs©® model because if you do take into consideration people's needs and wants you're more likely to achieve sales because you begin to sell them the relevant products or services for their needs. Knowing and using the criteria of our psychological model can help you target the right consumer group within your business industry.

I promoted this latter psychological human behavioural model which lean on what called behavioural science decision making and we already have one feedback from the LGBT community has one participant of this group identified with the third-level of the Girlfridayz psychological model of consumers' wants and needs—here's the feedback just after posting it on the 28-11-22 "Oliver O'Neill London, England -- Thank you so much for succinctly describing the LGBT+ community in your third level of the pyramid - couldn't have put it better myself."

See what effect the pyramid had on people the way it layed out play a big part to emphasised the trade off it exploit the view of the viewer and our brain compute it straightaway and identify with it immediately. Therefore, to achieve sales I would argue that you could present

Written by Trisha Amable – Girlfridayz – Website: https://girlfridayz.com
Girllfridayz number 10358020 girlfriday, girlfridayz™ is a registered trademark in the UK

a range of products or services using a pyramid shape infographic. The different approach of presenting the products with a short descriptive description will attract the consumers to purchase the product display or services if you attach a link and PDF the whole process, the pyramid will redirect them directly to your website. Here's an idea way too cool for school but excellent sales strategy an absolute killer strategy. If there is a stimulus between the sales happening and our brain will default to it straight away.

My idea is verify as it generates another feedback causing me to provide the explanative text. Here's the second feedback and my reply and all replies coming from NextDoor Neighbour, Linkedin users have not commented as yet.

EN from Pimlico "So how it differs from very basic marketing concept like 4p and others? And from when it became a 'psychological model'?"

I replied to EN "It's based on behavioural science this subconscious thinking leaks into conscious thinking and behaviour patterns are displayed very subtly which develops into habits and conforms to the person's reality and it makes sense in retrospect. It took me 15 years to put the behavioural patterns of human beings in this neat pyramid describing the Girlfridayz psychological model of consumers' wants and needs—which verify true with people and affects human emotions. Therefore bringing two decision-making processes rational and emotional. Knowing this every good marketer can offer perceived value to the customers to answer problems and meet their needs with products or services."

EN replied "really sorry but I don't see nothing new in this concept - everything is very well known and developed many many moons ago. But picture you created looks beautiful. But I see a discrepancy with some basic theories (eg., Maslow etc) and from marketing point of view I also don't see nothing new. But if someone find if useful it's ok"

I replied to EN this "It is not like Maslow's beautiful psychological model of human needs. However, Girlfridayz's psychological model of consumers' wants and needs is a new psychological model that validates human behaviour therefore you are right there is nothing new it is just validating beautifully how some humans are wired due to the second level of the pyramid and the rest of the pyramid flows from birth our behaviour developed depending on our upbringing and environment.

After working in health and social care for 15 years of my life many people displayed the pyramid behaviour and finishing my career as a registered care home manager, I studied behavioural recurring patterns in human beings and was able to articulate them beautifully in a neat pyramid matching Maslow theory proposition(1943,1954) where he stated that human motivation is based on people seeking fulfilment and change through personal growth. Self-actualised people are those who are fulfilled and doing all they are capable of.

I always thrive to be different and stating the obvious never feel new but confirm and validate behavioural patterns (Trisha Amable). I said the same in 2019 it didn't produce the same result in my blog post link to this post What Do People Want Most In life"

Written by Trisha Amable – Girlfridayz – Website: https://girlfridayz.com
Girllfridayz number 10358020 girlfriday, girlfridayz[tm] is a registered trademark in the UK

The difference lies in the presentation of the information display, the pyramid maximise the info' effectiveness.

A great deal of research is <u>undertaken to segment, target and position</u> (STP) customers by various criteria such as demographics, social class, geography and so on. From these marketers will have a very specific idea about who their target market consumers are and tailor their marketing strategies and tactics accordingly.

For example, a sweet manufacturer targeting young families is more likely to focus on young people and children in their advertising campaigns and on the cost of making their sweet healthy for consumption and abiding by legal and governmental regulations.

It is important to note that your target market's level or needs and desires may not stay the same, especially in times of political and economic change. Therefore, remember to keep your marketing strategy up to date and relevant.

A PESTEL analysis is a very important tool, and it helps you to determine the steps you should take in starting up or conducting your business and the bases for your SWOT analysis. It helps greatly to move your business toward the future and achieve sustainability in business for years to come.

Also using Maslow's pyramid in your marketing enable you to treat your customers correctly and access the right target market for your product or services by segmenting your market accordingly and your promotional adverts targeted to the right group of consumers for your products or services as you cannot market yourself to everyone in this life and every customer knows what they need and desire at any given time hence moving forward conduct customers analysis, survey and provide your products and services to whom is interested in what you have to offer.

It also helps you to provide what your customers' needs and wants are inclined towards being a business solution orientated for their customers.

Curiosity Marketing

Curiosity marketing is one strategy based on the natural curiosity of human beings. We as humans are naturally curious and will want to find things if people tell us information which makes us want more. Therefore, the conversation can be left in one line. An example could be your child's birthday and you planning a surprise birthday party. They ask you "I am having a birthday party" and you reply "maybe wait and see when your birthday coming".

The last part of the conversation "maybe wait and see when your birthday coming" arouses the natural curiosity that we have as human beings, and we want to know more.

You see how useful it is in your marketing to use curiosity marketing in your marketing to attract prospects or your customers.

Written by Trisha Amable – Girlfridayz – Website: https://girlfridayz.com
Girllfridayz number 10358020 girlfriday, girlfridayz[tm] is a registered trademark in the UK

Here is the one question which churned interest with most people.

We try this question on LinkedIn with our connection and we generated 100% positive responses. However, when you use this mighty strategy, you need to back it up with an irresistible offer. Here is the question below and our offer.

TA: I have an offer for you would you like to know what it is? (IO)

JA: Okay. Yes, I am interested.

TA: Okay that's great J follow by

I have a product marketing that may interest you Joshua (H)

I am Trisha Amable CEO of Girlfridayz Limited online marketing company, and we provide a wealth of Marketing services to SMEs in the UK.

Joshua has a marketing professional (TM) like us you might be interested in our Marketing Playbook the Core Assets of Marketing Revealed because it has been written for businesses to improve their existing marketing to increase their revenue over time by learning how to market themselves to the right audience for their products. (RW)

We believe Joshua has a Marketing entrepreneur you are a highly success-driven individual looking at your headline on your message you strike me as an individual who will be attracted to strategies which can improve your existing marketing to help your customers group small businesses to achieve greater. (B) (RW)

Joshua, if you purchase our Playbook I guarantee(G) you that you can master and learn strategies that are worth 10k to you and it will benefit your customers as you will be equipped with powerful strategies at your fingertips. (B)(RW)

We recommend that you read inside our Marketing Playbook to make an informed decision if you are not convinced that you could increase your business profitability by 10k Joshua. (CTA) https://www.girlfridayz.com/it-all-about-you

This post that I posted on LinkedIn to one of my connections uses curiosity marketing and inbound marketing to draw my connection into the offer which is now personal to him because I am using his name in the body of the Irresistible Offer which is to read inside this very playbook.

The response we got from various connections with the one question offer is mainly "thank you, Trisha, what the offer", "I love you Trisha what the offer" I sent it to a Marketing director "What the offer please tell me "Or "Trisha I want to hear your offer."

Do you notice how people's curiosity is aroused naturally, therefore, curiosity marketing has to be used sparingly and your irresistible offer needs to continue arousing the interest of the person therefore it needs to be something of value to the prospect or your customer and you need to make them see and believe that if they purchase your offer, it will be beneficial for them?

93

Do not confuse this mighty powerful strategy with The Irresistible Offer discount. You need to back it up with an Irresistible offer and you can use the offer on the top offer to keep the person interested. You will surely secure a sale or a call to use your services or buy the product.

Another example of **the One Question** depends on the level of knowledge and insight you gain in your existing customers or target market prospect after having done a psychogeography Avatar.

For programmer: "I have one line for you?" this is industry specific question.

Existing long-term customers: "I have a Lil something for you?" attract younger customers with internet slang or a target market prospect. It is to be used if you know your prospect or customers and they know you and the value of your work.

Otherwise, you say "I have something for you"

Alluding Headline: "They did not think I could do it, but we've created the world's first..." This was used by me to indirectly call attention to and hint at The Cellar without discussing it at length when promoting this very Playbook and its Dual Implementation Support System – The Cellar in the subject line of my email marketing. This headline depending on the offer could create a marketing buzz.

When people click on the email title the email opens, and they see the below example in the email body. Here is the metric Posted on 23/07/20 at 12.10 am – open rate: 25 clicked CTA: 5 by 10.23 am on 23/07/20.

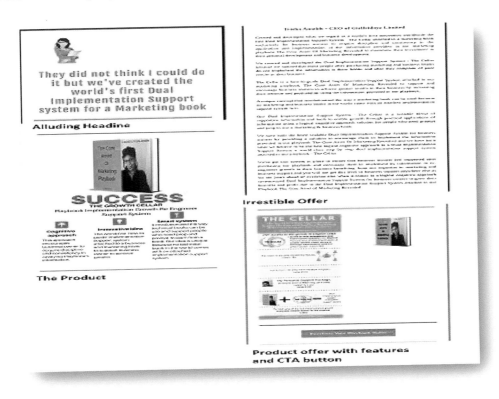

Alluding Headline

The Product

Irrestible Offer

Product offer with features
and CTA button

Psychographic Avatar is recommended for the curiosity marketing strategy you need insight into your audience and divide your audience into smaller groups or huge groups. In saying this you will find that the people you target relate to your product or services and they have similarities in their thought processes and can relate to your offer.

This is all based on the shared psychological characteristic including subconscious and conscious beliefs, and motivations explaining the predicted behaviours of consumers. This theory was developed in the 70s with its applied behavioural and social sciences to try to grasp consumers' decision-making processes, attitudes, values, and personalities. Lifestyle and communication preferences.

It complements demographic and socioeconomic segmentation and enables marketers to target audiences with messages to market brands, products or services, and lifestyle segmentation. Some marketers argue that it is based on consumers' cognitive style, which is sprung from their thinking patterns, feeling, and perceived value.

Communication

It is important when you run your business that you know how to speak and address yourself to an audience. The point of speaking to an audience is either informing or exposing, it is best when speaking to your audience to empower a promise by telling people what they did not know first and the reason why you are here. Do not put your hand in your pocket or behind your back, it can signal you have a weapon.

How to speak and address yourself to an audience

- Knowledge and application of knowledge (demonstrate your knowledge)
- Ability to speak.
- Ability to write.
- Quality of your idea
- Practice
- Talent (talent alone is not enough and seldom brings you success)

What matter is what you know and what you can improve on. However, having talent is useful; not be and all when it comes to addressing yourself to an audience.

If you have an idea about starting a business

- Imagine your idea (visualise it)
- If you express your idea in words, use verbal punctuation
- Distinguish your idea by putting a fence around it. Meaning does not discuss your idea with everyone because people can steal your idea or have a similar idea that you but not the same. It is best to be selective.

When you present to an audience in a large crowd do not start your conversation with a joke it is an audience turn-off at the beginning of a conversation.

Written by Trisha Amable – Girlfridayz – Website: https://girlfridayz.com
Girllfridayz number 10358020 girlfriday, girlfridayz[tm] is a registered trademark in the UK

Inspire your audience, use slides in your presentation and keep the text to the main point of discussion, remove the title, use bullet points, and short sentences. Use emphatic mirroring which is listening to your audience and seeing the world as they see it without judgement and trying to understand their feeling.

You can use graphic or image representation and prop to emphasise your points, demonstrate your knowledge and do not waffle be clear and engage your audience in your talk by moving your arm and hand, and using body language. Ask questions during your talk, not at the end which is a bad practice that people have the Q&A.

It is best to ask your question while you presenting which is called feedback loop to ensure that your audience is with you and participates. If you have a whiteboard, use a pointer to point at the information. It is good to use your imagination and imagine what you are saying.

It's good to build your style of presentation, you will come across as natural to your audience, tell a story people love a good story and try to persuade your audience especially if you try to sell something.

End a talk never said the end or thank you for listening to me which suggests that you are grateful that they came and spend their time with you.

You can end a talk by telling your audience how much I value your time and I salute you for that next time bring your friend when you come back again. Or you have been a fantastic audience and God bless you and Britain. You can tell a joke at the end. To inspire someone or an audience you tell them they can do it.

If you contributed to a subject list your contribution made to the subject in your slide but at the end of your talk. And remember above all it is what you know that your audience will be interested in.

When the road is blocked you need a strategy

We devised at Girlfridayz our competitor analysis which looks at the attractiveness of a business and the competition in a favourable way and not as rivalries like Porter's five analysis which looks at the external competition of a business the outside event that we cannot control and the logistic in your business.

The event, outside your control and family, your competition is after biting off big chunks out of your lifetime. From controlling the currency, and overcharging you on your gas and electricity use, utilities, food, and shelter, to siphoning your wealth, over taxation and political corruption these are all life events that most cannot control bringing out in people's distrust and withdrawal from others as they are no longer able to recognize who can bring genuine value to their life and affect business sales and quality of life.

Hence using the Core Assets of marketing to navigate people's negative inclination you need to use your positive mindset to bring the Core Assets alive as it is needed, and it has been written for the wealthiest mind who can recognise its magic and bring the genius in people

Written by Trisha Amable – Girlfridayz – Website: https://girlfridayz.com
Girllfridayz number 10358020 girlfriday, girlfridayz[tm] is a registered trademark in the UK

and has an eagerness to learn and improve their existing business or succeed with their new start-up.

Including the way your competitor used the most common marketing method of first making you feel inadequate and then conning you into believing that your desires are necessities killing you with features forgetting the benefit, they are all after the same thing: enhance the value of their own life by stealing away portions of yours.

Knowing this fact of life you need to follow your purpose your WHY you reading this playbook and your definiteness of planning and persistence, consistency and courage. You need to bring the Core Assets of marketing magic alive with an unshaken belief that you be successful and make the amount of money your heart desires and made up your mind that you will get the amount of money your heart desires as the Core Assets of marketing will widen your imagination bring out your infinite intelligence and infinite player attitude.

Historically the Girlfridayz Road Block Competitor Model Analysis©® concept created on 27/06/18 derives from Porter's Five Forces Model by Harvard Business School Professor Michael E. Porter in 1979 and the Marketing Mix 7ps by E. Jerome Mc Carthy and published in his book Basic Marketing in 1960.

The Girlfridayz Road Block Competition Model Analysis© is to support SMEs (Small Medium Enterprise) assess the nature of business competitiveness and develop strategies to suit their needs. The framework allows a business to identify and analyse the important driving drivers that consequently determine the attractiveness and profitability of a business in each market's external drivers and its internal driver by favourably looking at their competitors.

After studying these two business theories and our deep understanding of marketing theories and practices at Girlfridayz we were able to devise our own Road Block Competition Model Analysis, which was developed by Patricia Amable owner of Girlfridayz Limited in 2018 with the addition of People as they are the driving driver of any market and a business.

Defining the criterion People in Girlfridayz Road Block Competition Analysis Model means Employees, Leadership, Culture, Customers and Customer Service which is part of the 7ps of the Marketing Mix.

Girlfridayz Road Block Competition Analysis Model look at competitor analysis favourably and proactively not as a zero-sum game price war on who will win that narrow-minded game but more on the stance of the infinite player where there is no winner or loser but just looking at your business external and internal driving drivers in a holistic positive way and the underlining dynamic of your business.

You need as a business to look at your competitor for inspiration and growth as the larger company that succeed and are still thriving are the ones to admire as you know that their success did not come without hard work and belief in the Core Assets of marketing and knowing how to provide support to their customers to achieve longevity in business.

Written by Trisha Amable – Girlfridayz – Website: https://girlfridayz.com
Girllfridayz number 10358020 girlfriday, girlfridayz^{tm} is a registered trademark in the UK

You need to duplicate what they doing to achieve the same success or develop your innovation is good as people demand innovation that how the world progress.

Girlfridayz Road Block Analysis Model®© is a trademark in the UK and we recommend that you use it to conduct your competitor analysis.

After having studied Porter's 5 models of competitor analysis which focus on the external event that can happen in your business such as customer power, supplier power, the threat of substitute, competitor rivalry and buyer powers a method for analysing competitors in the business.

He based his analysis on organisation economics to derive five 5 forces that determine the competitive intensity and the attractiveness of the business in terms of profitability. He devised the logistic analysis of a business which is concerned with the delivery part of your business. Porter's strategies are good to use in your business.

Having looked at the Porter'5 model we saw a way to improve on its competitor model and devise the Road Block Competitor Analysis Model®© we decide to create Girlfridayz Road Block Analysis Competitor model as we have described above criterion and where our inspiration comes from.

It is possible to improve on an existing model for you if you see if something can be improved in any field hence if it is significant it is an adjacent innovation and it is good for your business as your innovation will be geared to help people and to support people achieve greatness with your tools so it is good to put your thinking cap on and look at the possibility to do and act on your idea to make yourself grow and acquire more customers which can generate business awareness, businesses enquiry and eventually if your idea is presented to the right people who will market it for you and spread it to the world.

You might be the next Bill Gate, Tim Benet-Lee, Thomas Edison, or Steve Job all these people got something in common they use their imagination plus specialised knowledge to create wonderful innovations that impact people's life positively and are here for years to come so think high and aim high you will only see who sit at the top and be inspired to walk in their footstep.

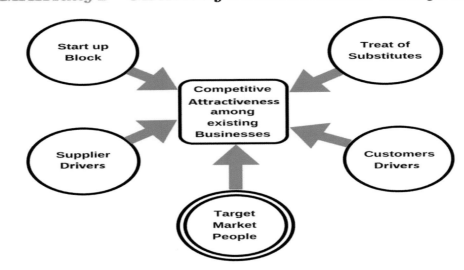

Figure 5 Girlfridayz road block Competitor Analysis©

How to use Girlfridayz Road Block Competition Analysis®©

Girlfridayz Road Block Competition Analysis Model is based on the attractiveness of the market you are in and your employee, leadership, business strategy, company structure and company culture, and customer service.

Before using the Girlfridayz Road Block Analysis Competition Model you need to do in-depth Market Research about your industry. As it is important to know which industry you are in and its drivers.

If you did not do thorough Market Research about your industry and similar industry you would not be able to fully complete Girlfridayz Road Block Analysis, bear in mind that our analysis is good for products and services as Girlfridayz is a service-based online company. Here is an example, of how to use our analysis we will on this occasion use it on us because it's also demonstrating that it can be used on any business size as we are a micro business.

Example of how to use Girlfridayz Road Block Analysis Competition Model®©

Girlfridayz is an online company that sells Marketing Services to businesses. The services provided are Digital Marketing, Traditional Marketing, Business Support Website Design and Backup admin.

As of 2017 Girlfridayz acquiring momentum in the marketing industry and has an increased following on LinkedIn and over 34k website views.

Girlfridayz believes in challenging the status quo, is customer-centred and believes they are different in thinking and the way they challenge the status quo is by going the extra mile for people.

Girlfridayz is known to be authentic, friendly, and hardworking, focused on operational details, efficiency, and a continuous focus on new product development. This strategy has allowed the company to maintain its low costs over the years. At present, the company is gaining steady online brand visibility and business awareness.

Girlfridayz Road Block Analysis Competition Model - For Girlfridayz

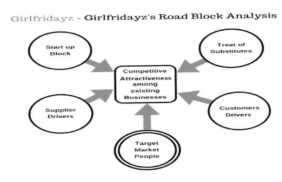

Figure 6Girlfridayz road block analysis model©®

Below you will find out how we use our own Girlfridayz Road Block Analysis Model® on our business and you'll discover our achievements and milestone achieved which are part of our business plan and marketing plan which are two great tools to have in your business has their purpose is to highlight your plan for your business success.

External drivers

The threat of substitute products or services

for services offered by Girlfridayz is high. This is because there are many services available that can satisfy the demand for marketing, business support and website design. Also, it can be argued that an increasing number of online applications and internet-based products and services represent an indirect substitution for a certain type of products and services offered by Girlfridayz but mainly an advantage also a threat, for example, the increasing popularity of self-servicing type base internet-applications and internet-based products as customers can self-serve themselves and design their products and services.

Attractiveness among existing businesses

There is significant competition in the Marketing Business, Business Support and Website Design market with the like of VistaPrint, The Local Authority which offers a free business plan and business advice and other local players such as Rich Vision who offer similar services or the same as Girlfridayz and mighty successful.

Girlfridayz believed if you cannot beat them join them therefore Girlfridayz is part of the Vista Print reseller program and is Government Accredited by the department of work and pension providing business plan using their template and guide, Starting a business online including business support and their CV service for people returning to work or starting work as well as acquiring a business award Be Mogul recognising the Most Influential & Inspirational Black

Business Owner in Britain by its direct competitor in the same industry marketing. Hence Girlfridayz has looked at its competitors favourably and acquired a business award and government accreditation.

Girlfridayz has managed to differentiate itself by maintaining a low cost over the years and going the extra mile for its customers and providing an excellent service to its customers and an excellent customer's service, being authentic, informative, offering an excellent quality of services to its customers and being true to their belief also challenging the status quo.

Start Up block: The threat of new entrants is low as the market is saturated and even if the requisite expertise is not difficult to replicate and financial investments are significantly low. The online business digital marketing and traditional marketing model require knowledge and expertise in marketing both in theories, strategies, tactics, marketing mix, business models, market knowledge and analysis, website design, business support and interpersonal skills. In addition, the market is saturated enough with the existing players that there is little attraction for a competitor large enough to threaten Girlfridayz's position.

Customer drivers: There is enough competition in the market to afford some power to the customers in the industry. Since Girlfridayz has built up its core belief around its competitive prices and offer value for money and is customer-centric. Customers can choose to switch if there is a sharp increase in the prices and favour Girlfridayz's pricing structure and service provision due to excellent customer services and pricing structure. There is little switching cost happening, though loyalty may be a factor that prevents a switch in favour of Girlfridayz.

Supplier drivers: Suppliers do not have substantial bargaining power as there are many options available to Girlfridayz around the world. There are numerous online applications and internet-based products and services that have the requisite expertise to partner with Girlfridayz. Despite this Girlfridayz attempts to form long-term strategic partnerships with suppliers which benefits both supplier and the company and works in collaboration with other businesses.

Internal drivers

Target Market People: Girlfridayz currently has one employee and in terms of leadership the owner is the CEO of Girlfridayz and manages all aspects of the business and its processes. Has Girlfridayz grown a requisite for staff may be required soon and Girlfridayz only wants 5 mastermind staffs' infinite players who believe in Girlfridayz vision and purpose as they are an online business and uses the technology available to provide their services? Girlfridayz's leadership, business strategy, company structure, company culture and customer service is embedded within Girlfridayz company which position itself as customer-centred, openness, transparency, authenticity including freedom of speech, diversity and inclusion are part of Girlfridayz's core belief.

Analysis of finding

In terms of business size, Girlfridayz is, a private limited company and fits in the category of small business but has the maturity of larger businesses well established in terms of business

101

processes, business policies and steadily gaining brand awareness online, offline and brand visibility mainly on social media platforms, which resulted in higher profile views and website visit increased. Due to the sheer volume of competitiveness in the marketing industry, it can be difficult to achieve profitability, but its attractiveness is high due to the general thinking that marketing is easy and there is a few exit barriers to consider, however, marketing is a science and require knowledge, skills, an ability to navigate market positively and undying belief in its application and the Core Assets of marketing strategies and tactics works to generate sales and bring you success and profitability over time.

The Step you should take before performing the Girlfridayz Road Block Competition analysis®

1. Gather information on each driver

During the first step, the company should gather information about their industry using the six drivers as a guide for classifying its information and use the diagram picture to ensure they follow the driver criterion to complete the analysis correctly. Be as accurate as possible this will support you to see the area of improvement or need and help you set further business goals for growth in your business.

2. Analyse results and display the diagram

After substantial information has been gathered, a team may sit down and analyse how each of the identified drivers affects the company. Every company will have different drivers affecting it differently. You must not make a comparison with other companies or use other companies' data it must solely be based on your business.

3. Formulate Strategies based on conclusions

The analysis of drivers affecting the industry can now be translated into specific strategies to further the interests of the company.

It is beneficial for a company to:

Before starting using the Girlfridayz Road Block Competition Analysis Model® to:

➤ Understand the goals of the analysis and expectations from it.
➤ Understand the scope of the analysis and who are the potential beneficiaries.
➤ Allow open and honest brainstorming sessions regarding these questions.

During the process of using the Girlfridayz Road Block Competition Analysis Model®

➤ Keep a focus on the future.
➤ Do not focus on what could have been done better in the past but focus on future improvements.
➤ Analyse the positives and negatives of company beliefs.
➤ Be open to new ideas and possibilities.

After using the Girlfridayz Road Block Competition Analysis Model®

- ➢ Identify lessons learnt and how they can be used in the future.
- ➢ Document positives and negatives. Identify best practices.
- ➢ Understand whether the analysis had the required impact.
- ➢ Follow up on implementation plans.
- ➢ Record information from the analysis to be used in a future decision.

When to use Girlfridayz Road Block Competition Analysis Model®

- ➢ To be used when there are at least three or more competing companies in the market.
- ➢ Consider the impact of the government on the industry.
- ➢ Consider which stage in the lifecycle the industry is.
- ➢ Consider the changing nature of industries and markets.

Girlfridayz Road Block Competition Analysis is a very useful, valuable tool and addresses the external driver's attractiveness by seeing the positive they can bring to your business and internal drivers of a business Girlfridayz Road Block Competition Analysis Model® can be used on any businesses size as the external and the internal drivers are affecting any businesses as Girlfridayz experienced. The only requirement to use our tool is when you have at least three or more competitors in the same market.

The power of positive words

What we say is what we get that is why we have added in the Core Assets of marketing this information for you to understand that you need to have a positive mindset and attitude plus develop a good habit to experience success in your business.

☞ our thoughts affect our circumstances so do the words we say to ourselves or posts on social media or letters written or spoken to others or ourselves.

☞ our words dominate our attitude, and they determine what we will attract and experience in our businesses and our life.

☞ the word that we use are always filtering into our subconscious mind and become part of the character and our makeup.

☞ our subconscious feeds our conscious mind and translates into behaviour and habits knowing this develops a good habit and cultivates a positive mind and you will develop a positive attitude toward life and other people.

☞ our words affect our performance therefore work hard toward what you want to achieve, with consistency, a strong desire to succeed, and discipline in your application of the Core Assets of marketing and you will acquire money.

☞ the word we say affects our memory and our subconscious is closely linked to memory hence positively talking to yourself, hoping and imagining your creativity will be developed and you will produce amazing.

☞ knowing this fact positive autosuggestion word spoken to self is needed to progress to succeed to recall.

☞ affirmation is a positive thought that you repeat to yourself daily and to make true and part of your genetic makeup.

103

👉**for your mental attitude; an affirmation**: Every day I am getting better and better and better at making money and my business is successful due to this.

👉**for your prosperity affirmation:** I feel healthy, I feel good, and I feel prosperous and thankful for all the support I received in my business to bring me to where I am today.

11 painful truths – fear not and success is in your grasp.

1. The words you think determine whom you are affecting memory and subconsciousness including consciousness.

2. What we imagine, and desire strongly happened.

3. Who you are is defined by your thought you shape your attitude and behaviour as well as habit.

4. We tend to attract what we expect.

5. Life only pays you what you think you are worth.

6. The only person who stops you is you.

7. whether you think you will succeed or not you are right (henry ford) the only thing that limits your achievements is your thoughts.

8. you do not take risks you do not prosper.

9. until you are committed to success the chance to give up is inexistent.

10. Whatever you can dream, or do ... begin it boldness has genius, power, and magic in it (Goethe)

11. You do not make mistakes you do not know what not to do and you do not develop problem-solving ability.

An attitude of gratitude in business is needed.

When you achieve success either be small or mighty be grateful and see what you have achieved and thank the people who brought you to where you are as our minds work and began to see what you have achieved in your business to continue enjoying this success you need to show gratitude and appreciation as an attitude of gratitude ensures that our attention is on what we want to achieve as we see ourselves as living abundantly and richly and recognising what we have to achieve set up a flow of good things coming our way as more often we found ourselves in the right place at the right time we need them. Also never forget your roster of the people who helped you on your journey of greatness be thankful and grateful and will acquire a tone of customers toward your business.

Business Goal brings your vision alive.

Written by Trisha Amable – Girlfridayz – Website: https://girlfridayz.com
Girllfridayz number 10358020 girlfriday, girlfridayz[tm] is a registered trademark in the UK

"Life asks of every individual a contribution and it is up to that individual to discover what it should be" Viktor Franki

Franki, in his classic book, "Man's Search for Meaning", wrote of his life in a concentration camp during World War II. He calculated that only one person in twenty-eight survived the horror of the camps and he made a personal study as to why one man survived while many others perished.

He observed that the person who survived was not necessarily the fittest or the healthiest or best-fed or the most intelligent. What he found was that those who made it through had a reason to keep going. They had a GOAL. In Franki's case, his burning desire was to see his wife's face again.

You need a burning desire to achieve your business goals to succeed because it is only then that you will know how to achieve them. Goals are what keep us going and pull us towards our overall vision when you achieve one note it in your business plan as a milestone and set another one and another one until you reach your vision and with a burning desire to succeed you will find that you never give up until you reach your destination.

Be a Nelson Mandela go all heartily after achieving your goals, made it your cause, and purpose and sail greatly toward glory he got the freedom that he wanted for his people and his country what a mighty goal, but he achieve it. This is the power of having a burning desire and imagination which enable creativity and a fearless attitude alive, courage comes in the face of adversity. This is why Madiba is the most regarded leader in the history of man.

Writing down your goals helps you memorise what you want to achieve cut them down into objectives and you are more likely to achieve them and act on them. There is enormous power in the list. The list gives you method and structure in achieving what you want for your business, therefore, the list becomes your plan and the definiteness of planning brings success.

The Limitation in your Business is you.

"Whether you think you will succeed or not, you are right - Henry Ford" as the only thing that limits our achievements is the thought that we can't achieve. If you think I will succeed, I will do whatever it takes to succeed, I will work if I need to be successful, I will learn as much as I can to develop myself toward my success, and I will be as different as I need to be to reach my success, I can do it and I am doing it you will automatically achieve success over time. In your business to achieve this powerful thought that you need to repeat daily to yourself, you will need personal discipline and organisation which bring out success.

When Handicaps look for inspiration from the people who conquer adversity

Written by Trisha Amable – Girlfridayz – Website: https://girlfridayz.com
Girllfridayz number 10358020 girlfriday, girlfridayz^{tm} is a registered trademark in the UK

Whenever you doubt your own ability to achieve, it is worthwhile to ponder the obstacles that others have overcome. Here's one outstanding achievement to keep you going and spur you on it embodies what persistence looks like.

Abraham Lincoln failed in business aged 22, lost a legislative race at 23, again failed in business at 25, had his sweetheart die when he was 26, had a nervous breakdown at 27, lost congressional races aged 34, 37 and 39, lost senatorial race aged 46, failed in his effort to become vice president of the USA aged 47 and lost a further senatorial contest at 49 but despite all his failure Abraham Lincoln never give up on his political dream of greatness and his persistence paid off at the age of 52 when he was elected president of the United State and his now remember as one of the great leaders in the world history.

The moral of this is **"it is not where you start that counts, but where you choose to finish"** and you have many stories of similar demonstrations of persistence by great people who made it in our history book, Thomas Edison was kicked out of school and brought us the light bulb, Henry Ford the car, Tim Berners-Lee brought us the world wide web and the list goes on. Handicaps are a blessing in disguise if you choose to see them this way and use them as an incentive to do better.

Mistakes are learning what not to do.

Mistakes are feedback on how we are doing, and a winner makes far more mistakes than losers that is why they are winners as they never give up despite their mistakes but develop the ability of problem-solving and are getting more feedback as they continue to try more possibilities hence there is no room for failure but just temporary defeat until you find the solution.

We learn far more from losses than we do from victories as when we lose, we contemplate, we analyse, we regroup, and we plan a new strategy. When we win, we simply celebrate our win and learn very little if we rest on our win, another reason to welcome error is it keeps us motivated to find the solution.

To prove it here is the story of the legendary Thomas Edison one day he was interviewed by a gentleman and asked the inventor how it felt to have failed so many times in his efforts to produce the electric light bulb. Edison famously **reply that he had not failed at all, but rather successfully found thousands of ways how not to make a light bulb**. Thomas Edison failed 1001 times before he found that by placing a bulb over the light the electricity would not die and remain alive and the light bulb was born. That kind of healthy positive attitude towards mistakes enables Thomas Edison to contribute to the world by giving us lights which makes it one of the greatest inventions in history and rivals other inventions by far. So much so that the light bulb is symbolic of a great idea that we use this picture of the light bulb when we have great ideas.

Written by Trisha Amable – Girlfridayz – Website: https://girlfridayz.com
Girllfridayz number 10358020 girlfriday, girlfridayz^{tm} is a registered trademark in the UK

Newton discovered the law of cause and effect: in other words that for every action there is an equal and opposite reaction. We only get back what we put out therefore our effort is required to succeed.

It is important to remind yourself that this principle affects everything you do and every experience you have. We cannot beat the law you reap what you sow, our physical health, our mental health, our business success, and our relationship are each governed by the same equation which requires us "to pay upfront".

The fascinating thing about the law is that we never know quite when we will be rewarded and when we will receive the dividends of our time and effort. But the rewards always come and the uncertainty of their time of arrival only serves to make life more exciting. In addition, what you have in your life now is a result of the sowing you have been doing until now.

Commitment is the pylon of success.

You must be committed to your success to demonstrate what commitment means I will write a poem by W.N Murray which embodies what is commitment to your business, ideas for growth and success.

"Until one is committed there is hesitancy, the chance to draw back, always ineffectiveness.
Concerning all acts of initiative and creation, there is one elementary truth.
Ignorance of which kills countless ideas and splendid plans.
That the moment one commits oneself, then providence moves too.
All sorts of things occur to help one that would otherwise never have occurred.
Raising in one favour all manner of unforeseen incidents, meetings, and material assistance which no man could have dreamt would have come his way. " W.N. Murray

Commitment is a state of mind and thought sprung from a burning desire to succeed and a strong belief in achieving the goals and vision you have envisaged, it brings with its discipline, consistency, organisation, imagination, creativity, and an ability to do what you set for yourself and a healthy positive attitude towards problems solving generated through mistakes which provide the rope to success.

Understanding how to Sale Services or Products to your customers

Figure 7e E. Jerome Mc Carthy 7ps of marketing diagram

107

The first reason is we think with our eyes and the price of your services communicates the quality of your product or services. Once you understand that you decide which business position you want to hold either be cost leadership or differentiation, but I think there is a third category where you can decide to be is value for money set your price in the middle for the services or products offer and to do this you need to look at your competitor prices from the cheapest to the highest and do the average. That will give you the value of your price for the same or similar products or services.

The second reason is setting your price right creates brand perception and attracts the right group of people for your business perception is what drives sales. If you want your business to provide high-end good to your customers your product need to be of good quality or higher quality, durability and provide long-term value. If you want your business to be cost leadership, your good is of lower quality and may not be durable requiring the customers to purchase repeatedly the same product or services and provide value.

If you place your price as average, you will attract customers who like average prices, not the highest or the cheapest therefore your product is of quality but may not be the higher quality of the high-end product and provide value to your customer.

The third reason is that fine bone China must be beautifully presented therefore it requires skills and competency, knowledge, and ability to make the product shine and its benefit and feature should entice sales the same principle is applied to your services. If the product shines brightly it commands its prices and people thinks its value is of the highest price therefore the quality of the product is exquisite and uses fineness ingredient and materials.

Walk in Bond Street in London and see a shop displaying products with no price tag because the product commands its prices however it has a defined prices tag already but it is not shown to entice the richest customers group in the shop and generate enquiry about the price of the item.

You can achieve this strategy online too I know of an artist on LinkedIn Alina Ciuciu an artist who is highly talented in painting and her painting command their price, she displays paintings sold out to create envy in people and display unsold items without displaying price or asking people to buy as the product command its price, therefore, she generates a lot of queries about the price of such artwork.

The four reason is eyeballs to eyeballs and face to face you must look at your customers without staring and engage in a conversation not necessarily about what you selling as most people does not like businesses to talk about what they provide unless you are asked. However, you still can attract customers by designing a beautiful promotion using the Core Assets of marketing and remember customers' perception is the driver of sales and shape their belief about your brand.

If you need to pitch your business use the Elevator Pitch you aimed to talk about your products or services provided in 30 to 60 seconds maximum this method is very effective.

108

You can do this using video, but you need to do your Elevator Pitch in 2 minutes maximum or under. You can do this on social media with a tweet, write 228 characters only the information has to be succinct and informative and use the benefit only of using your tactic enough to arouse curiosity in prospects. You can use Instagram to do this too and acquire prospects and customers.

The fifth reason is that you must love what you provide either products or services as it will transpire into your products or services presented to your customers if they perceive that you love your products or services, they will be more inclined to listen to you and the value the products or services will provide to their life.

The sixth reason is you cannot pressure your customers to purchase anything will it be services or products again if your customers perceive that you are aggressive or pushy, they will not purchase your products or services even if they have an interest in them. Because most people do not like a pushy seller but prefer an honest conversation about the benefit and features of your products or services and a reason why it will be good for them.

Therefore, the more information about your products or services you will achieve higher numbers of sales because prospects love to know about what the products or services can do for them. You must show your prospect that you are trustworthy, authentic, informative, and honest therefore integrity is everything. You must be responsible and accountable for your product by ensuring that your product is safe and secure for consumption. For services ensure that you provide the evidence meaning what you say you do it and your service provided is the tangible proof of what you do and must define who is it for.

It is not recommended to lie to acquire sales as it will automatically backfire on you and your business reputation will go down the drain and might cease to exist due to customers knowing that you are untrustworthy and dishonest.

There is no place for shyness when selling your product or services you must be confident and knowledgeable about your product or services after all you provide your products or services to prospect so you should know what you provide and the benefit and feature it hold you decide to run your business and provide a service to other therefore being knowledgeable of what you provide is a must.

It is simple as this to achieve a sale you need to listen to your prospect, they will usually tell you when they can purchase your services or products if you treat them right, your prospect and customer will recommend you to others without you asking just because your approach was just right.

The seven reasons are that your prospect needs stimulation on occasion to purchase from you they might be interested but the price is too high instead of pushing or dismissing the prospect ask questions about their challenges and try to get in their shoe as understanding and showing empathy can bring sales.

Written by Trisha Amable – Girlfridayz – Website: https://girlfridayz.com
Girllfridayz number 10358020 girlfriday, girlfridayz^{tm} is a registered trademark in the UK

If your prospect during the discussion must be friendly and positive and you sound just like you were speaking to your friends and they reveal that they have financial difficulties you then can offer an incentive by offering instalment payment if your business permit like this you achieves sales weekly, monthly or in two months or even longer period and both of you are satisfied this can result in repeated customers as they will want to use you often when they need you and be loyal to you.

In other words, be polite and make your customers feel comfortable with you and ensure that the business is comfortable with the incentive given and it does not result in harming you financially as every business incur cost this cost need to be paid to your supplier if you want to carry on providing your product or service to your customers. Therefore, the Core Assets of marketing need to be used wisely to your advantage and ensure that you are not disadvantaged too by using the irresistible offer.

The eighth reason is that you do not pitch understand the need and concerns of your customers and be enthusiastic when selling has no enthusiasm you will get psycho resistance, and this is not good and hamper your sales rate.

The 9th reason is that your prospect knows it is always about them and not about you therefore the attitude display is WIIFM (What in it for me) knowing that you tend to show your prospect the benefit of using you if they don't see it no sales remember we think with our eyes and perception either right or wrong is the key to selling because you can even achieve sales if your prospect does not need your products or services you should generate interest in your products and services and you can stimulate a need for it by describing your product or service as essential in your prospect life.

The 10th reason is that you create your luck there is no such thing as luck if you do not believe that you are lucky you will not be able to attract luck because you believe that you are not. Therefore, this lack of positive thinking hampers sales rate because you will automatically think that you cannot sell your product or service and you will attract prospects who stumble upon you and need you by necessity.

The 11th reason is knowing the latter the prospect must be interested in what you have to sell you need to make them see the benefit of them having the product or service in their life and make them imagine that they need it in their life, therefore, ensure that your product or service description is juicy enough so they can imagine it in their life and see the value of it in their life.

The 12th reason is that you must use price strategy, they are important to use remember perception and we all possess this in us if we perceive and view the price of a service or product as high, we automatically placed the business as a high-quality brand and think that the products or services are of high quality, therefore, your products or services automatically acquire value in the eyes of your prospect. The reverse is also true if you offer cheaper or the cheapest prices for your goods or services you will attract prospects who see your brand as affordable or cheap.

Written by Trisha Amable – Girlfridayz – Website: https://girlfridayz.com
Girllfridayz number 10358020 girlfriday, girlfridayz™ is a registered trademark in the UK

This will attract the prospect who think the higher the price tag the higher the quality of the product or service is and what you will find is most people are like this and will work hard to purchase what you have to offer if they do not have the fund or if they have the fund, they will buy instantly as they see the value of your product or service. However, only 20% of prospects are like that.

Word of the wise even the richest of people money-wise like a fair price for the good bought so ensure your price is right. If it is too high even a billionaire would not buy it, you would soon find that most billionaires are frugal people the extravagant ones lost their fortune due to bad management of money.

The 13th reason is a well-rounded brand uses both pricing strategy in their business and have high prices on some products or services and other are cheaper prices for the services or the goods. The business that achieves this has the most customers because they attract prospects who can afford their products or services at a cheaper price and others at a higher price. You will attract 80% of customers who are like that.

The 14th reason is that you must think of the prospect purse when you sell your products or services, therefore, the cost leadership pricing strategy is used and the cheaper or cheapest your products or services will attract the frugal prospect who does not care about the quality of the product or service that much but there should be the quality added value and they must see the benefit of having the products or services in their life as it often a necessity for survival as you provide what we all need to live with. You will attract 100% of customers to your business.

The 15th reason is that your prospect are very clued up about products or services therefore on some regular products or services your prospect roughly know the price it should be for the services or products you provide bearing in mind that ensure success but that does not mean that you cannot differentiate yourself within that.

For example, if you sell bananas in the UK you might say a banana costs you 60p and your competitor sale it for 65p and the next competitor £1 and the next one £2 and the next one £3 because banana only grows in a certain part of the world usually in the Caribbean and Africa where the weather is hot enough for it to grow the value of the banana may increase in price as it is imported in a country where it does not grow but remain cheap because it is a banana and it is widely available and it is seen as a product essential for the prospect survival, therefore, should be affordable to 100% of the population.

The differentiation in banana price can be it is a small yellow banana that tends to taste like an apple or green banana or yellow banana and remember depending on the product age the value either increases or decreases or the difficulties in acquiring this product make its value increase or if you create a product innovation is value may increase as it is new to the market but if it's an improvement on a product adjacent innovation its value may increase because it is a new product introduced to the market as an added value to what already exists it's what calls the differentiator in the product.

111

Written by Trisha Amable – Girlfridayz – Website: https://girlfridayz.com
Girllfridayz number 10358020 girlfriday, girlfridayz™ is a registered trademark in the UK

With any pricing strategy used thorough market research need to be conducted to get the right prices for your products or services as it will give you a rough idea of the price, you decide to charge for your products or services in your chosen market, your niche, and the industry you select to provide your business in hence benchmarking yourself with your industry.

When selling to a prospect engage the prospect in a conversation to get as much information on your prospect and use a feedback loop (such as does this make sense) by saying little think like this in your speech you keep the prospect engaged and use open questions to keep the prospect going as the more you know about your prospect it will be easier to sales your products or services to your prospect. The close question does not engage the prospect as they required a one-word answer yes or no. The open question provides engagement as an example: examine this dialogue with a business who attempted to sell me Bitcoin starting on LinkedIn Message then continued on WhatsApp **What not to do when selling your service to persuade a prospective client herein?**

Your products or services should have a name associated with the product type and your product should have information on its label or the product itself it is a legal requirement and this information help your customers be more informed about the product and its ingredients if it contained ingredient, its mechanism and functionality.

It is good to develop a full user manual about the product as it helps your customers use the product especially if your product is difficult to build or to use depending on the difficulties your user manual can be long or short with a diagram demonstrating the way to build the products or use it, it also good when writing your user manual to think of blind people and asked someone to do a version of it in braille, therefore, it will provide accessibility to this group of people and if you are thinking of selling international it is good that your product manual is in the country language. Also, for disabled people either physical or mental and to make your product accessible to them too and deaf people access to all people, this way you will have a wide range of prospect queries and customers.

Figure 8 Girlfridayz gap reduction strategic action model – your internal resistance to change©®

There are various selling methods, and some are subtle and do not require speaking to your prospect or customer you can present your product in a catalogue with a good description and information about the product and the picture of the product and use the Core Assets of marketing with your catalogue which is a great way to access customer and if you had an order form to it you can achieve maximised conversion as you add card payment too.

Hence people can order your product and pay for it then you deliver it. You can do the same for services and add a picture of your choice who represents your services, place an order form, and add card payment. as well as your website details and where people can find you on social media.

As an example view, girlfridayz catalogue of services is a novelty devised by Patricia Amable CEO of Girlfridayz 5th/09/2019 to improve distribution channel online as we find we widely encounter mainly products displayed in the catalogue and they are printed version and sent

Written by Trisha Amable – Girlfridayz – Website: https://girlfridayz.com
Girllfridayz number 10358020 girlfriday, girlfridayz^{tm} is a registered trademark in the UK

to consumer home Girlfridayz find a gap in the market in the distribution channel available to our disposal using our own Gap Reduction Strategic Action Model – Your resistance to change©®.

Our idea of services catalogue is very simple but fantastic is different it does not contain products but only our services and can be downloaded and save on your computer and all links are clickable back to our website page where the pertaining service can be found and viewed as we are an online business providing online services and soon, we want to have our service catalogue printed to distribute offline as it is currently available and accessible online.

It is a good distribution channel and can be adapted to product display as part of customer maximisation giving the prospect the best of both worlds use email marketing to distribute your product catalogue they look at it and jump back to view your e-commerce site and purchase a targeted product as you direct the prospect to the relevant page of your products.

Especially good if you have many products to display. You can limit the number of products on your online catalogue and put the most popular or the least popular to make them shine or if you are a local shop with a small product selection an online catalogue displays your product and directs people to your shop saving you the cost of printing.

Technology permits to use of both mediums you can have an online product catalogue in PDF format to download with targeted links to the pertaining page of the product even down to the product checkout system.

Catalogues allow you to display a maximum of products and can vary in size and the number of pages does not matter a great deal if your product is informative and beautifully display you will achieve sales as well as your website details and where people can find you on social media. Technology permits to use of both mediums you can have an online product catalogue in PDF format to download too.

Flyers also can be used to display your product or service on a smaller scale, but it is effective as well, you can place an order form on your flyers too if you display a product or service as well as your website details and where people can find you on social media maximum conversion.

You can sell your product on an e-commerce website and display physical goods and e-goods for download and your services are the best displayed on a business website.

You can sell your products on Google Marketplace, Amazon, and eBay all these businesses allow you to display your products or services for a fee as you are using their platform to achieve sales.

You can use Facebook's shop to sell your product directly from Facebook if you live in America but for other countries, you can still set up a shop on Facebook, but your checkout will redirect to your e-commerce checkout. You can display your products or services on social media

114

platforms and redirect your customers to your website by ensuring that you insert a backlink in your post or tweet. You can sell from your blog and add a PayPal button to get paid.

Figure 9 selling your product internationally diagram – Girlfridayz.

Honey Luscious Strategies

When you have a website and sell your products and services online, there are strategies that you can use to up your game and couple the 9 Core Assets of marketing with it you will manage to up the number of prospects visiting your website and increase sales over time.

1. In-demand products

Be sure your products are in demand in your target group. There is a saying in marketing. If you are selling pasta, there is only so much you can do if you don't have a hungry crowd, in other words, the better you get at aligning your products to the hunger of your crowd, the better your sales will be. Meaning ensuring that your products are aligned with your target group or changing who you target.

Written by Trisha Amable – Girlfridayz – Website: https://girlfridayz.com
Girllfridayz number 10358020 girlfriday, girlfridayz[tm] is a registered trademark in the UK

2. Great Product descriptions/images

You like to read nice descriptions when you view people's websites well the revert is equal, most people like to imagine themselves having, using, and owning the product. Do your product descriptions help them see the value of each product in their lives? Make sure you describe both benefit and feature as the feature defines the benefit and include inspirational pictures that help with buying decisions.

3. Free Delivery

It is no secret that the words "free delivery" are a major sales converter. Many customers become accustomed to it, and this can work at your disadvantage if you give too many discounts because you think you will acquire mighty sales.

Therefore, on your website, it is good to give balance to your website the free delivery irresistible offer as to be used strategically meaning it should not be a permanent feature in your website but on occasion, this is what you offer to your customers.

4. Free returns – credit note – product replacement – alternative product

If your customers are not happy with their purchase, you need to offer a free return. Before you do this, you need to see if you can sort out the problem your customers tell you about and give them a solution.

If your customers his still unhappy with your product you can give a free return of their products and offer a product replacement or an alternative product and place a credit note on their account to ensure further purchase and referral as if you do this word of mouth will spread.

You need to manage the cost of return and therefore ensure that you provide to your customers an excellent service to minimise the free return option – credit note – product replacement – alternative product. Because too many costs can hurt your business and happy customers ensure return business.

5. Pay later options.

This incentive on your website is good to implement as some customers prefer to pay by instalment and managed their payment as it is easier for them and both benefit from this option therefore a win-win strategy.

Because this strategy is to be devised online you need to pre-qualified your customers and ask them to fill in their details as part of your repayment of purchase contract once they are satisfied with your condition, they are happy with the term and conditions you deliver the product and enable automated payment weekly, monthly payment via debit card or credit card and direct debit.

Written by Trisha Amable – Girlfridayz – Website: https://girlfridayz.com
Girllfridayz number 10358020 girlfriday, girlfridayz™ is a registered trademark in the UK

6. Competitive price/ value for money

If your product matches your competitor, it is up to you to adjust your prices if you wish to because having the same prices as your competitor for the same services gives choice to the consumers and if you can differentiate yourself too by having the price slightly up or down to give you a 1 up that could be the differentiator tactic.

7. Great deals/discounts

It is amazing how your customers love discounts worldwide and jump at the chance to get a cracker of a deal would be Halloween, Valentine's Day, International Women's Day, Cat Day, Christmas, Easter day and any other celebration day. People just love a good deal. Therefore, come up with plenty of seasonal discounts to grab your customers.

However, this irresistible offer tactic can backfire on you as too many discounts can harm your business and you not making any profit as you cannot manage the cost of your business. **Example of discount tactic**: Limited edition, 24hrs sales, by one get one free, buy two for the price of one, buy three get the four items free, bonus with your purchase, get a percentage off your purchase and so on use your imagination and create irresistible deals.

Here is a cost recovery tactic when you want to offer a substantial discount to please your customers you cannot do it to your detriment too therefore increase your price by 20% or 40% then apply the discount amount you want to offer.

Here is a delay discount tactic when you want to offer a substantial discount amount to please your customers, but you cannot afford it you set a condition or conditions to get the discount offer on a service or a product of interest. If the customers meet your condition, they get a discount.

At Girlfridayz we inserted a hidden substantial discount in <u>Fred our Statutory redundancy calculator</u> if you find it you win money off an e-commerce website design. We also use gamification marketing we have a game lifewithmore#win that we bring out yearly if you win the game, you get a discount on one of our services.

The above tactics and strategies are win-win strategies because they benefit both of you as your customers get a substantial discount and you also recover your cost. Very versatile tactic and strategy and can be applied to products and services.

8. Reason to Buy now – not later

You need to give your customers an incentive to purchase your product straight away hence presentation as its importance therefore this is linked to your description of your product and the feature and benefit of using your product plus a supportive picture will entice the customers to buy the product now and this is online therefore it is easier to implement.

117

If you have a brick-and-mortar shop as well as an online presence your reason to buy now than later is your brick-and-mortar displays the product look good the shelves are neat and tidy and the product is easy to be found as customer perception is important and the first impression count.

The décor theme of your brick and mortar attracts your customers too as they will love your display which has to be practical and ensure safety to your customers.

9. Customer reviews of you as a merchant

Offer a review of a product or e-good social proof good or bad helps you improve your customer service, and it can help you acquire more customers. Whether be you a start-up or an existing business you need to uphold good customer service.

10. Fast checkout

Install fast checkout processes on your online e-commerce if your customer has to fill out a long form or too many details they have a chance to abandon the cart, therefore ask for delivery information or an alternative address for delivering the product and if it is a download you need to capture the same details which are name and surname, address details, postcode, telephone, email.

11. Subscription to your email marketing

Install this option on your online store and if you use this line never miss an update or access our sought-after content by subscribing to us you get a discount offer and good content. An incentive for people to subscribe to you. You cannot pre-tick your form and you need to display this message by submitting your information, I agree to your [business name] to handle the information and upload your data policy and which includes the cookie policy. It is a legal requirement.

12. No pre-sale registration or exclusivity

You can have two-way access to your site; the no pre-sale registration is for instant purchase of your product your customers view it and by it this most used option worldwide. However, you can create exclusivity if you have a membership club and what you offer is for its member only and you can sell a product within your club to your member.

13. Mobile-optimised checkout

Ensure that your e-commerce online store can be viewed on your mobile phone too and that your checkout function is the same on your mobile as on your website. If you manage to do this, you can increase sales on mobile.

Written by Trisha Amable – Girlfridayz – Website: https://girlfridayz.com
Girllfridayz number 10358020 girlfriday, girlfridayz[tm] is a registered trademark in the UK

14. Immediate recognition

It can welcome your customer to your store by stating their name Hi Trisha here you can pay by visa, this helps sales and your customers feel nice. You need to create a customer account at checkout to capture your customer's details.

15. 24 hours sales

With a sizeable discount of 90% of the price offer for 24hrs only. Only use this strategy for High products and high prices too as if your product is well known or sought-after you achieve an enormous number of sales in 24 hours. If your product is good but has less notoriety you can pull this strategy with a smaller percentage amount but juicy enough to entice.

Remember this above all else

Interpersonal skills lead to success and organising your thought into practical steps that will lead you to your goal is necessary, you need a burning desire to succeed, consistency, discipline, patience, and taking a positive risk to help you and your decision-making process do not give all you have for free, value your worth, your skills, knowledge, and ability.

Human beings value what has a price, what is free is usually disregarded as a universal weakness of ambition, specialist knowledge, knowledge and highly specialized knowledge required payment according to your skill, knowledge, and ability. Hence the irresistible offer tactic need to be used sparingly.

Bonus content to keep the prospect attentive.

1. CREATE A LANDING PAGE

Landing pages are one of the most proven ways to build your email list and attract visitors to your product or services. These website pages are for driving potential customers, to purchase, sign up to your blog, read articles or visit the rest of your website as they also serve as entry pages of a site.

Building your email list usually requires you to use a lead magnet and it uses the strategy of reciprocity marketing you are asking someone to give you their personal details in exchange for valuable content which provides a solution to their needs. These can be free guides, factsheets, videos, small e-books any valuable content that you can afford to give away for free.

These landing pages are used in very specific ways and can be part of a lightbox, banner or whole page website, accessed by form or button, text link and usually contain a CTA.

Services like MailChimp, ConvertKit, and more provide such features for their users to design landing pages aimed to collect emails.

Written by Trisha Amable – Girlfridayz – Website: https://girlfridayz.com
Girllfridayz number 10358020 girlfriday, girlfridayz[tm] is a registered trademark in the UK

Congratulations!

You've been selected for the next round of free gardening sessions at the Hathaway Park!

Enter your email to get a free indoor gardening guide and an invite to our next public gardening session. And as a thank you, we'll also send you a **50% discount** on your next order of gardening supplies.

Email Address

2. CREATE A HOMEPAGE SIGN-UP BOX

Depending on the kind of website you running and the type of website you may want to screen access and require visitors to sign up to your website before viewing your content, these are very useful for client account creation and return visitors to your website, if you have an online store they are perfect to capture returning visitors or business website if you have a personal website and you want to create an exclusive club online use a signup procedure.

3. CREATE A WELCOME MAT

A welcome mat or opt-in form is useful to acquire an email to build your email marketing list and contact your prospective customers they usually have an opt-out option to give your visitor the choice to opt in or out. It provides a double conversion as if a visitor clicks the opt-out or no thank you button they can be taken to view your blog or another product they may like. Be careful not to stock the customers in a loop and the only way to come out of it is to purchase something or download something.

They can also be snack bar notifications which just direct a visitor to a piece of content which you think might interest them. The cool part is you can present this page in two ways:

Scrollable: Once the visitor sees the Welcome Mat, they can simply scroll past it and see your blog post. Once they do that, though, the Welcome Mat disappears and is inaccessible.

Instant Landing Page: If you want to force a choice, however, you can turn the Welcome Mat into an instant landing page. To get to the blog post, the visitor either gives you their email address or clicks the No Thanks button.

Habits shape your business growth.

The habit of a wealthy mind: The importance of persistence and there are baby steps to snap out of mental inertia. Cultivate the habit of persistence and you get rewarded plus knowledge of how you get there. Do not be defeated by the silence of the power that comes to you through persistence as we have nothing to fear except fear itself.

Persistence is a state of mind which bring out the definiteness of purpose, self-reliance, discipline, consistency, patience, and courage as willpower lead to persistence resulting in habit and repeat of courage give you a new life you soon find who you are.

The subtle power of persistence is defined by the mastermind principle as when people work for the same common goal and purpose, people take on the power of thought to the people they associate with and share beliefs or similar beliefs by achieving success through a positive attitude, emotion approach merely passing judgment on it will not bring benefit.

"We are continually faced by great opportunities brilliantly disguised as a problem until we learn the solution something is perceived as hard as perception plays a great deal in our win or failure" Trisha Amable.

You need to use your knowledge, or you lose it this principle is applied to everything in our physical and mental health. If you do not use the knowledge learned you lose your touch, use your creativity and imagination. In addition, when you stretch yourself, you become more courageous, and we develop strength by regularly testing ourselves.

We need to keep caring about ourselves and the things that matter and keep using our minds to keep in shape there is no reason why we should become less able as the year goes by. If we keep on using our mental capacity to the full, our minds will keep working for us.

The same principle applies to money, money needs to be used it needs to circulate, you need to spend money in your business to make money, and you need to use the money available that you have — therefore have a budget, keep reinvesting your capital and take positive risks.

How to make your business profitable

Hot profitable tip:

Here it is 11 easy steps to follow to make your business profitable over time do not forget to use the Core Assets of marketing combined with one or more strategies to get there.

1. Charge your prices and do not offer too many discounts as it chips away your profit potential.

2. Segment your audience and your niche, as you cannot sell your services or product to

Written by Trisha Amable – Girlfridayz – Website: https://girlfridayz.com
Girllfridayz number 10358020 girlfriday, girlfridayz^{tm} is a registered trademark in the UK

everyone.

3. Find the right audience for your product or services and relate to their need by providing a solution.

4. Apply saving costs in your business but not at the cost of your customer's welfare.

5. Enter sound investment after doing solid research because it is not all investment which is good for your business.

6. Do not borrow money unless it is necessary for business growth and you know you can repay the debt swiftly in less time possible because the longer it takes the higher interest it will generate.

7. Treat your customers as you want to be treated with respect and care and do not assume what your customers want but asked questions and engage them in a meaningful conversation.

8. Qualified and disqualified people aim for quality input rather than quantity.

9. Follow up on customers' purchases, and offer aftercare packages as well as related offers

10. review underperforming suppliers meaning do not stay because of loyalty.

11. Increase your price yearly by 2.4%

Storytelling in marketing is a winner all around

The handbook of Reflective and Experiential learning from Jenny Moon (2004) helps you to self-reflect on experience and refers to it as reflective learning, and you can express your experience as storytelling in varied mediums to engage your reader and analyse your feeling or encounter with customers or prospect your business experiences and this process can help you acquire more prospect and convert them into customers.

The process of reflective learning is a guided selection of events or issues focussing on the consideration of the following:

- Observation
- Comment on personal behaviour
- Comment on reaction/ feelings
- Comment on context

Additional resources for you to pounder on could be fed into your idea of reflective learning storytelling as follow:

Written by Trisha Amable – Girlfridayz – Website: https://girlfridayz.com
Girllfridayz number 10358020 girlfriday, girlfridayz[tm] is a registered trademark in the UK

- Further observations
- Relevant knowledge, experience, feeling, intuitions
- Suggestion from others
- New information
- Formal theory
- Other factors such as ethical, moral, and socio-political context

Reflective thinking occurs when you are processing and relating your experiences or experimenting, exploring, or re-interpreting from a different viewpoint or within a different contextual factor, theorizing and linking theory and practice, and cognitive thought processes.

Other processing may occur such as testing of new ideas in practice and/ or representation e.g.: your first blog draft, infographic or discussion. This leads to a product result of something learned or you feel a sense of moving on, or you may feel the need for new questions and further learning.

Using the process of reflective thinking and learning at Girlfridayz we were able to recount several encounters with prospective customers and use various mediums to convey our stories and reflective thinking which may attract you to use the same strategies highlighted in our stories to further your business growth as everybody loves a good story.

Story one: When you speak to your right audience whatever you market to them may work in your favour providing that you know how to sell without selling and not pushy be patient and get to know your customers by having a conversation, the right approach, friendly, positive, and professional.

In our reflective thinking and learning, we were able to recount in picture storytelling How to Nurture Your New Customer to Ensure Business Longevity. We posted this story on our LinkedIn feeds and Facebook page and our story attracted a small amount of engagement as we used a graphic representation of our story.

It is not the graphic per se which may not have encouraged more people to read it, it is because LinkedIn picture size allowed compromised the number of views it was first designed with a huge size because we wanted people to fully grasp the context of the story and see the strategy used to achieves this amazing results with our customers and these people are still how customers and we think we share this with you in this very playbook. Because in your business you encounter many people, and you experience good and bad customers or prospects in your business life.

Therefore self-reflective processes are mighty useful to update your policies, and processes in your businesses, implement security, become stronger within and devise strategies as you review personal behaviour and changes these innate behavioural pattern which works to your advantage or disadvantage as we experience at Girlfridayz or remember your best encounter with prospect and how you get as your customers and remember the relationship in the process with your customers without losing professionalism and boundary that business requires to prosper.

Written by Trisha Amable – Girlfridayz – Website: https://girlfridayz.com
Girllfridayz number 10358020 girlfriday, girlfridayz[tm] is a registered trademark in the UK

How to nurture your new customer to ensure business longevity

In 2015 I was promoting my business giving my business card and three fold brochure to the local in my neighbourhood. I visited the local garage next to my office. They knew I lived in the area for years and the garages are there for years too. I went in the second garage and spoke to the owner and offered to do a wall banner to promote his business. He said yes and the wall banner design is still on the wall to this day. Here the story in picture how I nurtured my new customers and got referrals.

Banner fitting

Supported my new customers to fit his banner on the wall free of charge as a neighbourly gesture and while talking I said do you like your design he replied yes. I say you will increase traffic to your garage with this banner showing your services and contact details.

A year gone by

Being friendly like I am I start talking to the guys at the local garage and spoke to R the most as well as the staff of C and every xmas I gave a diary and a pen with my business on it.

Rescuing his computer

I diagnosed what was wrong he had a virus and no anti-virus installed. I manage to see his file. I back them up on a portable hard drive that I told him to purchase.
Them re-installed Window 7 for him. Once the job done I installed several programs and restore back up and told him to run his anti-virus program regularly.

My friendly talk about anything with R got me referrals

R has my marketing material pin in his garage board for years. One day I was at his garage talking and he had a friend there, who asked about my business in July 2018 and hire me to do his music website in December 2018.
You can view our website gallery. https://www.girlfridayz.com/website-gallery

C new banner

The local and his customers start discussing his new banner on the wall and saying you finally got your banner done mate it's a prime location too, and the first garage R went to see C and asked who done your banner he replied Trisha next door.

In 2017 Home Office Bell Ring

C at the door panicking. I say what up he replied my computer no longer work I know you can fix it Trisha can you come please. I say ok I am coming I have free time and C call my phone next time. He replied yes I got your number. I said you do — use it please. He said Ok

Referrals for computer maintenance coming in

Next in 2017 I fixed a lot of computers for the local. C surely spread the word Trisha fix computer, Clean them up and back them up for you and update your operating system. and I still do.

2018 contacted C

Told him hi C, how are you. He replied fine Trisha and you I replied I'am fine, I said I was looking at my window your old banner still holding but ain't you tired of the design it been three years. Do you fancy a new one. He replied send me a what's app sample please. He has the new banner and it not up yet. I guess he love the old banner design.

Source •Girlfridayz.com – trisha Amable CEO – **https://girlfridayz.com/it-all-about-you**

Further reflection on story one as a coincidental twist as I posted this picture story on my social media on 5/05/20 C fitted his new banner and hired me to remove virus from his computer here it is below my reflective learning:

Regarding my story about my long-term customers, he finally fitted his new banner on 5-05-20. I delivered it to him on 31/01/19 that was so coincidental. I just posted on LinkedIn How to nurture your new customer and left my office and C was fitting his huge new size wall banner, plus a spare one on the railing.

Written by Trisha Amable – Girlfridayz – Website: https://girlfridayz.com
Girllfridayz number 10358020 girlfriday, girlfridayz[tm] is a registered trademark in the UK

He said good job you came outside my computer playing up. I took his computer to my office Google Chrome was infected by a PUA and was redirecting to Bing, but the URL was funny. The PUA virus takes your browser data and saves them and sends them to the thief should he have put his bank details and checked his account online they could have logged in after him and stolen money.

I removed Google Chrome and waited for a safe version after advising them of the infection and installed it for my customers' AVG safe browser which looks like Google, but it is AVG.

(PUP) or potentially unwanted application (PUA) is software that a user may perceive as unwanted. It is used as a subjective tagging criterion by security and parental control products. Such software may use an implementation that can compromise privacy or weaken the computer's security.

Story 2: The Benefit of Attending Business Event

In this reflective thinking process about how we acquired a business award and, in the process, highlighting the importance of networking as you never know where it might lead you in our case it got us a business award (The be mogul award 2018/19) titled Recognising the Most Influential & Inspirational Black Business Owners in Britain by the Be Mogul Team. A radio interview and advertisement opportunity on the Be Mogul Magazine as well as a column about our business and me the CEO and owner of Girlfridayz.

The format of our storytelling is a short reflection writing and we used our award video to support our story.

The Benefit of attending a Business Event

On 23/11/18 I collected the Be Mogul Business Award Recognising The Most Influential & Inspirational Black Business Owners in Britain in the NatWest Bank venue.

Here is the story, back in 2016 on LinkedIn Mavis A from Rich Vision posted her event coffee morning with Mavis business event.

I reply and got my ticket from Event Bright. I love the way she conducted her event and the business information provided was so helpful.

I continued attending several events by Mavis and Rich Vision team. I attended the award ceremony of the award winners of 2016/17 and after the event, Mavis asked who want an award for the next year 2018/19. I collected my form and fill it and give it back.

In 2018 I received an email telling me that I was selected for an award, and could you please tell us about your business and any adversities overcome and income?

I completed the form, and send it back. On 1/11/18 I received an invitation to attend a radio interview with Mavis business talk ABN radio Norwood.

126

I attended and find myself on-air talking business with Mavis all the nation could hear me. Then she told me I was the winner of a business award the judge selected girlfridayz.com

You see it pays to attend business events and network with people.

This reflective story posted on my LinkedIn attracted 69 views and one comment "Dynamic person all standards" Ahmad Nuwaila. The small amount of view is due to the retargeting of my award video with my short reflective writing about the benefit of attending business events because I have posted this very video on various platform back in November 2018 and just used it as a supportive medium for my short reflective writing to re-enforce the truthfulness of my story.

Story 3: The Benefit of Promoting Your Business

Is a reflective piece of writing about meeting a small business shop owner back in 2015 he became my friend as well as my long-term customers and word of mouth referrals started coming in all through 2015, 2016, and 2017 and still to this day he refers me if somebody asked about any of the services we provide. We have posted this on LinkedIn to encourage small businesses to use a direct pitch conversational strategy to acquire potential customers and this post got the most views out of our three reflective writing stories about how we acquired customers and a business award.

127

Written by Trisha Amable – Girlfridayz – Website: https://girlfridayz.com
Girllfridayz number 10358020 girlfriday, girlfridayz[tm] is a registered trademark in the UK

Here it is below:

The Land of opportunity back in 2015 I was promoting my business in my local area. I walked into the Mama Jai shop selling African food mainly Nigerian.

I met with the owner and offer to design a website for the shop he said yes but not for his shop but his other business in Health & Social Care. We completed his website https://lnkd.in/dPW6Tia.

He was so pleased with his website and functionality that he asked me to design a second website Perfect Property and the three-fold brochure for his Health & Social Care business.

Why the land of opportunity I also became his backup admin and he used our admin services for 5 years now.

We even became friends and I got so many referrals and recommendations for my business from Mama Jai he referred me to the family, friends, and his church, plus his best friend computer guru became my friend too and the three of us wanted to set up an internet cafe together (that still in the pipeline)

You see when you do excellent work for your customers and you are friendly, positive, professional, and fun they become your advocate for years.

Want to experience our friendly services and start your own story with Girlfridayz.com call us at 07931089744 visit our website and pick the services that suit your needs.

Analysis of my last reflective writing storytelling you will get to learn about our mistakes and what we learned from them including my reciprocal marketing deal which grew my business 10 times folds.

In hindsight, I should not have gone as far as I went with my relationship with the owner of Mama Jai, and kept more on a strictly professional level as our business relationship went murky, to say the least even if we are friends to this day and he still used my services when he needs them.

I came to the shop with an irresistible offer for the owner of Mama Jai's African delicacy store. The original price of his business website was £350, and I offered to him after a discussion over the price a discount of £100 off and say £250 and I do it for you. He replied yes you hired and requested a payment facility to pay for his website design.

We did not offer this service at that time but to secure the order we say yes and told him we have a payment facility for services over £200 he qualified for it, and we will send him a confirmation of the order with the payment schedule enclosed. He replied yes.

Written by Trisha Amable – Girlfridayz – Website: https://girlfridayz.com
Girllfridayz number 10358020 girlfriday, girlfridayz™ is a registered trademark in the UK

We went to our office and updated our website with this new service as we thought it was a brilliant idea for people who have a low budget and therefore could acquire more customers this way. We updated our pricing policy with this new service too.

My new customer was so pleased with his website and impressed with the functionality of his website that he hired me to design his three-fold brochure for his other Health & Social Care business. We designed his brochure he was so impressed and like us. He told me that I am friendly, approachable and have a great sense of humour. I replied thank you.

As time progressed he contacted me for admin work, and we had to come to his shop to do his admin. He was happy to have me around, he offered me a deal that I could not refuse. He said that I could work from his shop no rent to pay him and could get prospective customers from his shop. I discussed this with him thoroughly and said we have an office he replied, that it would be far better for you. I agreed as we needed exposure.

I started working in his shop for free helping with his customer's sales and tidying up the shelves, doing the delivery and collecting his payment he was the local supplier for blessed West Indian Shop, however, every customer who wanted my services he let me have them and do their works and get paid for it through my business Girlfridayz.com in my office.

He even referred people to me on a regular, the church people, his friends, family and in turn I looked after his shop and I increased sales in his shop he was over the moon as I was promoting his shop for free, putting advertisements designed by me on his window for free.

This is what is called reciprocal marketing my customer base grew 10 times over and his customer traffic in his shop doubled due to my friendly personality and approach plus my laughing and joking nature. He was so happy with our arrangement that he lost sight that I was a business too and he viewed me as his friend that he loved.

The local neighbour noticed the increased traffic and come to his shop to ask questions about his competitors. He never said anything significant enough to jeopardise his business, so they started asking me questions such as you are working for him, I replied yes as well as Trisha you are doing so much for him do you want to work in my shop? I replied no, my boss would not like this, and my business associate loved this because our reciprocal deal was confidential and part of the deal was, that he is not to divulge to anyone our business deal to which he signed our contract this effect.

Christmas 2016 I got invited to the shop Christmas party by that time he considered me part of the family, and his friend R my good friend now the computer Guru, called us the three musketeers and try to use us for his advantage, so we called him a cunning person he does have this trait in his personality.

For Christmas that year I gave him a free 5 pages analysis of his business and how to improve his customer base, and shop look to attract more people. He loved it so much that he said it is the best present someone did for me in 30 years of running my business. I got Jollof rice and a bottle of wine that Christmas.

129

Written by Trisha Amable – Girlfridayz – Website: https://girlfridayz.com
Girllfridayz number 10358020 girlfriday, girlfridayz[tm] is a registered trademark in the UK

He implemented some of the recommendations and the shop look better tidy and customer magnet. He improved his open hours and start opening in the morning like his competitors and put a notice no more credit was allowed because people could take 10kg of rice worth £24 and walk out of the shop and say we pay you in a month and we see them in two months or never return and he was complaining about people dishonesty.

Hence, I was pleased that he stick to it and his regular customers noticed the change and we discussed it in the shop. It did take some people time to get used to the change in his behaviour and new resolve.

Mama Jai's owner was so pleased with our friendship and R the computer guru asked me if I had another business which one would it be. I replied, an internet café with 5 computers, and we served tea and coffee with cake to the customers.

R said yes shall we do it the three of us set the network and the computer. Trisha, you installed the software checked them and promote the internet café, Mana Jai owner we use my shop at the back I got space I can clear up the place and we share the money with the three of us.

The intention was there we got to plan the internet café, R brought the computers and set up the internet connection, I installed software and designed promotional materials for the internet café and requested payment for my services and Mana Jai owner paid me all my money.

R requested payment for the computers he refused to pay him on the ground that he was his friend for 30 yrs. I helped my friend R to get his money and eventually Mama Jai paid him but by drip, all the money owed £300 as Mama Jai got the computers cheap due to his long-term friendship with R. R was ok with this because he was his friend and I told R in business there are no friends you sold your computer dirt, cheap mate.

He replied it is ok I replied do you not value your skills, experience, ability and worth. He replied people always want cheap Trisha, I replied it is because you allow them so they do it and added the day you say no and go elsewhere people will respect you it is because they know you are very kind and they take the piss R.

Time passed and we were in 2017 our reciprocal deal marketing continued, he asked me to design another website, perfect property for his lady friends with benefits and I charged him the discounted price of his first website £250 by then our website prices had increased therefore he had a substantial discount.

I completed the website and he had signed all his documents too; he was happy with his design of perfectproperty and the functionality. Here's when he lost sight of business and became personal.

Written by Trisha Amable – Girlfridayz – Website: https://girlfridayz.com
Girllfridayz number 10358020 girlfriday, girlfridayz™ is a registered trademark in the UK

He fall out with his new lady friend with benefits and refused to pay me for the website he ordered. I replied it is too late to cancel and you are liable to pay for your order you have approved the website and still must pay the deposit I requested I want my full payment now.

I went to my office and devised my cancelled policy and send it to him via email and cancelled his payment facility. Send him his signed documents and attached a demand of payment for service completed. I also designed our working agreement and other various policies we did not have on our website. Also, our business had grown 10 times folds too and we had lots of customers and prospect queries.

He was so shocked, to say the least, he said you are my friend Trisha. I replied in business there is no friendship and you lost sight of your business mojo, I have not, therefore, my full payment is due, and I will not hesitate to refer you to the small court to collect my payment.

He was vivid and cancelled our reciprocal marketing deal. I replied fine you owe me £250, and you will have to pay regardless. I got cussed and I cussed him back, see how this got murky. I stood my ground and a week later after he come down, he decided to pay for his website by instalment and told me £5 per week via email.

I replied fine I draft your arrangement and if you miss one payment the whole agreement is cancelled. He replied fine and for a year and four months, I collected £5 per week every Saturday until he finished.

He never used the website perfect property but paid for it. After this, he still called me for admin work, design, and printing work up to this day, but he must pay me upfront now. He asked for our reciprocal marketing deal again I refused because I have a good insight into my customer and I managed to keep everything professional between us up to this day, even if we are friendly with each other.

He also learned that there are no friends in business and R too because now every time Mana Jai owner asked him for a computer, he must pay upfront and R bring the computer to him.

In hindsight, I can see professional boundaries got crossed but I gained so much in terms of business growth, and I devised systems and processes for my business during these five years and have implemented a non-discount strategy because too many discounts take away your potential profit.

We became more sophisticated as a business much stronger in our resolve to achieve our overall vision, we got limited status, got a trademark, a business award and UK government accreditation.

If this reflective story helps you in your business that is very good because, in business, you must always uphold professionalism.

My customer took my kindness for weakness and got shocked when he realised that all along, I was dead serious and that I had entered a beneficial business deal for both of us.

131

Written by Trisha Amable – Girlfridayz – Website: https://girlfridayz.com
Girllfridayz number 10358020 girlfriday, girlfridayz^{tm} is a registered trademark in the UK

How to sell your services as a branded product

COVID19 has devastated the UK economy, and the country just exited the EU on 31/01/21. Two major economic events impacted greatly small businesses and large businesses. Our business Girlfridayz managed to survive the pest and we access a COVID19 grant to help us survive. We got awarded a small sum of money from Facebook COVID19 grant for small businesses.

The Lockdown has shut down many businesses due to fear gripping the world over catching the deadly COVID-19 virus. New jobs have been created and the sales of face masks, hand sanitisers, app restaurants, and online businesses selling clothes and other essentials item thrive. Supermarket shops increase their revenue.

However, marketing companies for businesses start-up and growth services declined, hairdressers, and other industries' products or services were nonessentials during the crisis; closed temporarily until permission to re-open is granted. There are numerous online marketing companies and due to the perceived value that it is easy. However, marketing is a science as well as its applications.

Girlfridayz Marketing needed to differentiate and make our online business shine. The marketing industry marketplace is crowded, and we needed to be considered as a valuable brand to use its services as any other products or services available amongst the sea of competitors.

Here is what we used to make our company Girlfridayz Limited as a branded product providing Traditional and Digital marketing to start-ups and SMEs and individuals.

We used 7 Core Assets of marketing with one strategy (Psychology marketing perception), and we use Porter's 5 logistic model and attractiveness of a business, Girlfridayz Road Block Analysis Model©® as well as Ansoff Matrix. Ansoff Matrix is a strategic planning tool that provides a framework to help executives, senior managers, and marketers devise strategies for future growth and UX design concepts taking into consideration our target market (prospects and customers) and our offering (marketing to business). We wanted a competitive advantage by penetrating the market, and diversification and we wanted our brand to be perceived as a product available in the market.

GIRLFRIDAYZ' CUSTOMER JOURNEY OVERVIEW
HYBRID-BRAND MULTICHANNEL

Meet Girlfridayz's multichannel, where expert award-winning result orientated services are broken down and rebuilt anew. This epic expertise mapping in a way that empowers Startup & SME's to grow their business through grasping that the services work closely interlink with your customer's need.

Services Buying customer Journey

https://girlfridayz.com

 Brand visibility

 Prospect, Customer, entry point

 Services done for customers

DISCOVER
**Social Media.
Search, Reviews
Word of Mouth**

CONSIDER
**Research
Learn, Call us
Testimonials**

PURCHASE
**Online purchase
Store Purchases
Order form Purchase**

UPGRADE CYCLE
SME's Business Services, Online Presence
Social Media Marketing, Admin Support
Planning, Print Marketing, Lead Gen, survey
Advertising, Directory Listing

SETUP
**Startup Business Services
Online Presence
Social Media Marketing
Admin Support
Planning, Print Marketing
Advertising, Directory Listing**

LEARN
**Blog Articles, Local Event
Business & Marketing ebooks
Business & Marketing Self-contained Courses
Marketing Playbooks, Cellar Membership**

SHARE
**Word of Mouth, comments
Reviews, Referrals
Social Media, Friends, Associates**

Feedback
Testinomial

ENJOY
**Reading our Blog Articles
Listening to our Podcasts
Using our Business Tool Calculators**

MANAGE
**Website Maintenance
Yearly Website Maintenance Subscription
Plans Updates, SEO
Blog Updates, Creation
Social Media Management**

EXPERT SERVICES
**Website Design, SEO, copywriting,
Website Migration
Planning (Business & Marketing)
Social Media creation and update
Social Media Management
Lead Generation, Business Goal
setting, Business Support services
Graphic Design, Admin services**

SELF SERVICES
**Online Booking Appointment
Creating your accounts
Sign up for Deep Pockets Loyalty Program
Online Payment for services ordered**

Girlfridayz
Business support
for sole traders
and SME's

133

Written by Trisha Amable – **Girlfridayz** – Website: https://girlfridayz.com
Girllfridayz number 10358020 girlfriday, girlfridayz[tm] is a registered trademark in the UK

Customer Persona & Scenario Marketing.

Introducing Girlfridayz TIME Matrix©®. Our newest model uses 4 quadrants which are T I M E and **T** means Timing, **I** means Iteration, **M** means Multiple, and **E** means Engage when it comes to qualifying leads remember it's about time.

Each criterion is explained below in a series of pictures presenting our model and its use with Andrew's example customer persona and experimentation and introducing iterative Marketing. If you want to know what Iterative Marketing here is the definition. Iterative Marketing is a structured methodology for planning, executing, and optimizing marketing. It is independent of any technology platform, instead providing a set of tools and techniques for applying continuous improvement to your marketing activity.

Customer Persona & Scenario

Andrew
The Pet Owner

Andrew would like to find a pet groomer service for Cutie in London.
Related to the needs identify for his cat Cutie.

Andrew customer Journey

Key Things to know
- Microchip for Cutie.
- Clip her nails.
- Grooming her fur.

When it comes to qualifying leads — remember it's about time.

Timing | Iteration | Multiple | Engage ®

Summary and Primary Goals

It's pandemic time and cutie needs urgent nail clipping and her fur grooming . Andrew used his mobile phone to search for pets service in London South East where he lives. He found on Google The Groom Room but he is put off by the form. He continued is search and found Absolutely Animals based in South East London. He noticed that they are open and follow Government Guideline' about COVID19. He viewed their Facebook plug in and clicked on a post of interest. He noticed customers and people engaged with their content and they have good reviews on their website.

Iterative Marketing - Absolutely Animals

1. **Brand Discovery:** Andrew discover Absolutely Animals through search.
2. **Persona Discovery:** Andrew Pet Owner.
3. **Journey Mapping:** Andrew searched on google, discovered Absolutely Animals and found all information he needed to make an inform decision.
4. **Channel and Content Alignment:** Website with Facebook page plug in, twitter and Tumbler.
5. **Experimentation & Optimization:** Absolutely Animals offers shop visit, only 1 customer in the stop at any one time in response of COVID19.
6. **Reporting and Feedback:** Customers engagement and reviews on their website as well as their Facebook page.

The 6 components of Iterative Marketing

You can see our model Girlfridayz Time Matrix in the picture and to use it you need to display the model with its headline. The Time Matrix is composed of 4 green rounded square quadrants with each quadrant containing its relevant letter and meaning. The quadrant of Girlfridayz TIME Matrix® is Timing, Iteration, Multiple, and Engage. Girlfridayz TIME Matrix® is a strategic planning tool that can help you to prepare and respond to external influence to retain customers or acquire new customers.

Here is the picture of Girlfridayz TIME Matrix® below with an explanation of each criterion in detail.

Written by Trisha Amable – Girlfridayz – Website: https://girlfridayz.com
Girllfridayz number 10358020 girlfriday, girlfridayz^tm is a registered trademark in the UK

Girlfridayz's TIME Matrix®

When it comes to qualifying leads — remember it's about time

Timing **T**	Iteration **I**	Multiple **M**	Engage **E**®
Timing is concern with government influence, social trend, environmental influence and Customer needs.	Iteration is concern with the product's or service's content lifecycle and the customers, leads omnichannel, multichannel journey experience.	Multiple is concern with the multiplying effect of the strategy and tactics used in content strategy to attract the lead/customer to purchase from a business.	Engage is concern with the likelihood of the lead, customers engaging with a business content, purchasing product or service from a business and reviewing purchases.

Figure 10 - Girlfridayz's Time Matrix

We continue with the journey of Andrew our customer persona looking for a grooming service for his cat cutie.

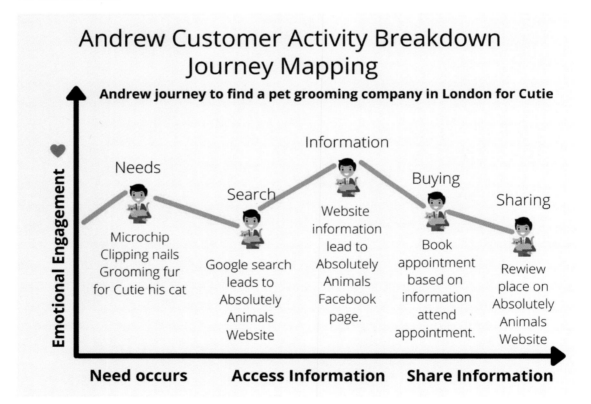

Figure 11 Girlfridayz customer Activity Breakdown Journey Mapping

Written by Trisha Amable – Girlfridayz – Website: https://girlfridayz.com
Girllfridayz number 10358020 girlfriday, girlfridayz™ is a registered trademark in the UK

In term of Absolute Animal, our company use Andrew's Customer Persona. He used their grooming services and they have completed a Customer Persona to target Andrew with related offers according to his previous purchase. Below is the experimentation of which offers Andrew will be more attracted to.

Figure 12 Girlfridayz Experimentation and optimisation

In your business when you acquire a customer, we recommend that you get a good habit and design a customer persona base on your new customer acquisition and their purchase of your service or product. It will help you design personalised offers tailored to the needs, likes and income bracket of your customers. You could after easily use upsell, cross-sell and down-sell strategies with a minimum of 6 to 9 tactics for maximum optimisation of your marketing impact.

Customer Persona and experimentation are very useful tools to use in marketing and you should use them frequently to ensure you send your targeted offers related to the perceived need of your customers based on their previous purchases.

Big businesses use them daily this is why you receive email or notifications or sales letters or on your mobile phone offer address to you and more than often enough you click or call or visit the company to see if the offer is still available or to use the discount.

I used our model Girlfridayz TIME Matrix® you can recognise the criteria Timing, Iteration, Multiple, Engage, in the example below of a one-time customer that becomes a return customer. Based on the information collected from the customer persona about W I could

136

Written by Trisha Amable – Girlfridayz – Website: https://girlfridayz.com
Girllfridayz number 10358020 girlfriday, girlfridayz™ is a registered trademark in the UK

retarget him with a related offer concerning his previous purchase. It works fine we got the job.

An example of this is 19th/04/21 I sent to the previous customer W that I designed a landing page for him 7 months ago. A free review based on his website design and what's app him {I} him the result of the review with an offer.

Here is the conversation:

"I W(TM), how are you? I built a website last year August 2020 {T} (H). I conducted a free website review and I noticed that you have updated the content (RW), however, the layout of your website has inconsistencies. Your anchor menu links spill out to a More button with an anchor to wallets and shops. You have a new page with no name, and it is blank… (explaining the RW I contacted him) We can fix all these issues easier for you and design a new page for £160. {I} (FB) We can offer you a 10% discount on your new page design should you want to use us again. This offer ends on 26/04/21. (IO) Yours sincerely, Trisha. (Sent at 18.01)".

He replied to my what's app this at 18.02 "Hi Trisha, thank you for reaching out. {E} I give you a call on Wednesday afternoon to discuss as there is a need to revise the contents of my site."

I replied 18.02 "Yes, call me around 2 pm if it is ok with you Trisha".

He contacted me and we discussed the design of his new page and the tidy-up of his previous one. He agrees to the price offer and give me the job. You see how useful it is to do a customer persona in your business you can acquire more sales from the same customer, no matter how long he uses your services or product.

Consider using customer persona with our Girlfridayz TIME Matrix® in your business regularly with your existing customer or even the one-time customers like my example above, he was referred to us last year by one of our regular customers, and he used our website services and ordered a landing page. I re-targeted him 7 months later with a **lead magnet** (a free website review) and **used 5 Core Assets of marketing {M}** (TM, H, RW, RW, FB, IO). The IO was a conditional offer (**I said should you want to use us again**). The nostalgia works like a charm and we acquire a return customer because he said during our conversation, I used you once why not twice I was happy with the job. I got a word-of-mouth review. (SP).

You see how useful it is to be organised in your marketing and use customer persona because you can acquire more and increase sales and profit.

Have you found the secret yet reading this Playbook?

Here it is we reveal the secret in this playbook Amazon are using the right marketing technique and method therefore they get the right result and you too can achieve this in a small amount of time with the same or similar result and maintain the result you are getting by using the Core Assets of marketing repeatedly as they are workable technique and method

Written by Trisha Amable – Girlfridayz – Website: https://girlfridayz.com
Girllfridayz number 10358020 girlfriday, girlfridayz^tm is a registered trademark in the UK

and use them to your advantage the result is visible and tangible as you can touch and feel the money you are making.

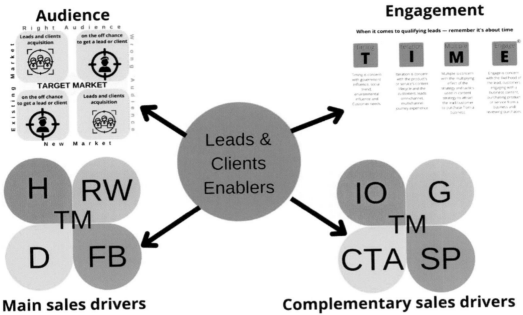

Voila, the well-guarded technique accessible to the selected few, the serious ones, the diligent, persistent, patient, and positive the ones who want to grow and known as time progresses, they are growing but they feel secure and believe in the subtle power of the right marketing technique and method because they are using the right tools a sharp one, not a blunt one. They are using the fundamental of marketing and its application to business.

The secret has been revealed!

There are not many just 11 strategies plus 9 tactics the Core Assets must be used with every single strategy preferably 8 tactics as Social Proof can be difficult to get, and you can combine any of them in any order you want. Using 2 to 3 tactics gets a poor result. Use the template to get Social Proof fast to be used with existing customers the one you sold one product or more or repetitive customers they are happy to give you a comment.

As every business is different but the Core Assets of marketing are for every business there is nothing different every business has access to the right strategies and tactics and can systemise them to become part of their business system therefore business processes and keep on using them to bring awareness of their brand and achieve business sustainability,

Having said that every business needs to treat the customer with support toward their need meaning you provide products or services you need to ensure that your services or products

Written by Trisha Amable – Girlfridayz – Website: https://girlfridayz.com
Girllfridayz number 10358020 girlfriday, girlfridayz^{tm} is a registered trademark in the UK

meet the need of the customers as when a customer is happy with your services or products they will refer you to other readily and willingly give you testimonial and referral they become your ambassador and championed your business for becoming the pylon of the community its operate in or becoming known worldwide as a good brand where people want to be associated with and the customer will pay you for the support given and their need met.

You need to work hard when you run a business and make a big effort to succeed the Core Assets and strategies are your tools to do so if you do not implement them within your content, I guarantee you poor results if you carry on doing what you are doing you will always get the same result.

It is easy to complain oh my business is not working; I do not have enough customers it is stagnant it is because you are not changing your marketing and you are not using the Core Assets daily and the 9 of them with the strategies to see a different result no you have become complacent, and you satisfied with mediocre results not trying to get better.

We can see that in businesses which have achieved success; they let go of the tool thinking that they made it and do not need them due to their brand name or their database of customers but gradually their businesses lose customers and money then we hear it's because of the competition or it's because of the economy, they will blame everybody but themselves full of excuses but if they look they have stopped using the Core Assets and the strategies or use 1 only mainly discount and one a day they are forgotten and disappears altogether and another business emerge as a replacement complacency set in and blame take its place that why.

You see the business that you hear saying this is 50 years we are in business or more years we are in business these businesses move with their time and the Core Assets of marketing are second nature they use the right technique and method all through their years and become sustainable through time example Sainsbury brand or Adler since 1949 it's not magic it's just using the right tool of marketing simple. They are easy no technical skills are required but creativity is required.

You just duplicate them simply because your competitor is using them you duplicate excellence if they are excellent, and you make it a new habit having said that you need to be creative and think about how you can differentiate yourself from your competitor your plus one. It is not rocket science just learning the technique and method. It is easy but if you are lazy and do not implement them and you have been given the right tools and not using them to your advantage it is not anyone's fault therefore you just take ownership and responsibility for your inaction.

Words of the wise: The person who stops learning merely because they think they know everything is forever hopelessly doomed to mediocrity. The way to success is the way of continuous pursuit of knowledge. Knowledge acquire must be put into use, for a definite purpose through practical plans. Knowledge has no value except that which can be gained from its application towards some worthy gain.

Written by Trisha Amable – Girlfridayz – Website: https://girlfridayz.com
Girllfridayz number 10358020 girlfriday, girlfridayz[tm] is a registered trademark in the UK

You purchase our playbooks and acquire the knowledge you required to improve your marketing, increase sales and over time become profitable. We guarantee you cannot fail as we have made sure that with the information learned if applied correctly failure is not an option.

We tested everything we wrote for years that why we are marketing experts and doubly qualified for that matter and won a business award and an accredited business. Develops your skills, knowledge and ability plus imagination and creativity and puts them to use toward greatness, with your imagination, and determination to grow you will be committed to your success.

It is important to have basic discipline in your business to be successful and remember It is not practised makes perfect but perfect practice makes perfect.

In other words, commit yourself to be successful and use the legacy system at your disposal in this playbook and they will become second nature to you. Look at metrics to progress it is important but do not get engrossed with metrics. Do not stand still and keep having a competitive edge over people to remain on top of your industry and always do your best.

To build a world-class business you need to build it scientifically using a proven set of time-tested parameters and methods and then add leading-edge tactics and strategies found in this playbook that produce results in acquiring clients by creating a dual business system for you and an implementation system for your client through using this playbook.

The Cellar is a Dual Implementation Support System attached to this Playbook.

If you want to use The Cellar Membership, you will need to purchase a membership package from our online store. We offer 2 membership packages 3 months, and 6 months, use of the Cellar Dual Implementation Support System attached to this Marketing Playbook.

You get access to the Cellar dual implementation support system via this:
URL: https://girlfridayz.com/access-to-the-cellar
You will need a password to get full access to The Cellar membership benefits and features. The password is **TheCellar02** enter this password to access The Cellar Guest Area and enter the Dual Implementation Support System for this playbook after verification of your details.

Earning Disclaimer

- You are not going to magically make 6 figures today or in the next few days, but you might see an increase in sales in two months or before if you implement the tactic and strategies in this playbook now. You know that it takes time, persistence, and effort plus consistency to get a favourable result.
- You will see positive results only if you work hard and use the Core Assets of marketing plus the strategies daily in whatever content you produce.

Written by Trisha Amable – Girlfridayz – Website: https://girlfridayz.com
Girllfridayz number 10358020 girlfriday, girlfridayz™ is a registered trademark in the UK

- Apply more of the system meaning when you find the strategies which get you results you systemise them and use them repeatedly as they are only 11 and 9 tactics systemised them all.
- A major transformation of your existing marketing technique is required, and you must use the Core Assets 6 maximum 9 better the strategies will get you results and only then you will see positive results fast.
- Whatever you can do or dream you...begin it. Boldness has genius and magic in it - Goethe.

Bonus content here below about the law of Attraction and if you change your mindset, you will gain whatever you want in your life and your business. The law of attraction is a philosophy suggesting that positive thoughts bring positive results into a person's life, while negative thoughts bring negative outcomes.

The Law of Sow and Reap

This is the law of **'sow and reaps'**, where if one puts in their best efforts to give themselves the best education, training and coaching today, one shall see results being achieved in times to come. Take, for example, one of the greatest politicians and visionaries America has ever seen – Abraham Lincoln.

Why You Are Not Getting What You Want

Whatever we want is at our fingertips; we only need to apply the right method to attract them. But if everything is at our fingertips, why most people in this world aren't happy with their financial condition, their jobs, their health or their love lives? Why do most people fail to build their ideal career, or business, attract their dream relationships, or start their way to earn millions? Indeed, many people never heard of the law of attraction. Others have some understanding of this law, yet still can't use it to achieve their dreams.

What is the law of Attraction?

The law of attraction is a science that is already in effect— we can either understand and align our behaviour to or remain ignorant of and suffer because of that ignorance.

Look at the reasons why most of us don't get what we want in life, and why the law of attraction doesn't work for us. It is because Reality Is the reflection of your inner world.

The world we live in is the reflection of our inner world. If your inner world is in harmony, you will experience harmony in the outer world. Everything will fit perfectly into place, and you will find your life in perfect harmony, gain clients easily, become prosperous and your business will thrive.

Contrarily, if the inner world is in disharmony and is dominated by negative emotions like fear, anger, frustration, doubt, hate, and guilt, life will feel like a constant struggle. You will experience defeat, lose faith in yourself, and choose a life of limitation.

141

Written by Trisha Amable – Girlfridayz – Website: https://girlfridayz.com
Girllfridayz number 10358020 girlfriday, girlfridayz[tm] is a registered trademark in the UK

It is hard, sometimes impossible to change things that happen outside, but it is very much possible to change what happens within. The law of attraction won't work for you if you fail to bring your inner world in harmony and start thinking positively.

The Cycle of Failure

Failure is an inevitable part of life. It's a necessary part of life, which is critical for our self-growth. Every time we experience failure, we should accept it and move on. When we fail to accept our failures and start anew, we unconsciously reinforce the belief that we deserve failures.

As our negative belief grows, we keep focusing on failures. We direct all our attention to how to avoid failures, rather than to how to pursue success. Consequently, the law of attraction gives us more failures because we are unwittingly asking for it. In this way, our negative beliefs become irresistibly powerful, and we start to accept the fact that we are destined to fail. Unconsciously we expect defeat, and it becomes a self-fulfilling prophecy. As a result, we become trapped in a vicious cycle of failure.

But if we had a positive core belief that we would be successful, and that belief was reinforced by successful incidents, our subconscious mind was convinced that we are meant to be successful, and as a result, we attracted success.

See what is happening here? We're shaping our future through our beliefs. It is our deep-rooted beliefs that bring forth all the negative or positive incidents we confront in our daily lives. And this process follows the simple rule, '**like attracts like**", "**we are what we eat**", and **"you are the process of your thought"** because there is no limitation to the mind except for those we acknowledge.

However, sometimes even a positive mindset can fail to bring the desired result. Here are the reasons why the law of attraction fails even if you have a positive mindset. It is because you don't have the willingness to **Do What It Takes**.

Simply believing in your dreams won't manifest things for you. Achieving life goals or Business goals requires action, determination, grit, belief you can achieve it, consistency in speech and action and commitment. If you're unwilling to do what it takes to chase your dream, you won't be able to attain it.

Patience is required

To manifest something, you must trust the process. Manifestation can take time. If you lose your patience and give up, the process will stop. Therefore, trust your vision, trust the process, and wait patiently.

Don't spend too much time anticipating

Getting what you want in life or your business or achieve business growth using the law of attraction is simple— set your intention and become clear about what you want, belief in your abilities, knowledge, skills, and yourself, believe in the universe, practice manifestation

Written by Trisha Amable – Girlfridayz – Website: https://girlfridayz.com
Girllfridayz number 10358020 girlfriday, girlfridayz<tm> is a registered trademark in the UK

techniques, and keep working on your goals. The universe will do the rest. If your dream is too big, it is normal that you to make assumptions about the possible ways the universe can make it happen. Let the universe sort this out. Just hold the vision in your mind, continue to work on your goals and wait patiently. The vision will become a reality in no time.

Smart Aleck or not business ideas come to your head

Society has developed and implemented creative concepts to solve problems in our lives and improve the way we are living. These progressive ideas are called innovation. There are two types of innovations adjacent innovation is to create a new solution to an existing problem to a product or service or infrastructure, on the other hand, a direct innovation is to develop and implement a new product that never existed for example Sophia the first AI Humanoid robot.

She is also the first Humanoid to be granted citizenship in Saudi Arabia and got first place for UNDP's innovation. As another example, The Cellar is a mentoring online support system attached to The Core Assets of Marketing with its Dual implementation Support System – The Cellar a technical marketing book. The Cellar is the first mentoring online support system attached to a technical marketing book.

There are two types of innovations either tangible or intangible. A tangible innovation is a physical product; however, an intangible innovation is non-physical but visible and mainly called theories in product development or marketing and its business application.

As an example of intangible innovation, The TIME Matrix strategical marketing model is an audience attraction theory for a product to be accepted by the consumers and its marketing journey through marketing channels to bring awareness to the consumers about the product's existence and the review of the said product. Throughout this book, you can use Girlfridayz 9 intangible innovative theoretical marketing models to apply to your business to acquire leads and sales.

Innovation in your business is needed to grow your business. You do not have to be the business creating the innovation or you can be the business creating the innovation. However, you can use the innovative bots by embracing the development in AI (Artificial Intelligence) that large businesses use to improve their system thinking in their business.

Robots are used in factories that make the factory fully automated for the automotive industry and require fewer human resources for the performance of repetitive tasks and some complex tasks. However, on the scale of your small business, it is recommended that you use bots in your social media marketing. In Facebook Messager, WhatsApp, and SMS messages for example this will cut down on your query time for prospects and customers.

Nevertheless, you should use bots intelligently meaning only use bots for routine question ask about your business and the answer is always the same. Do not use bots for specific questions and answers that a prospect or customers can ask about your business, products, or services. Because it is best to use inbound strategies and talk to people in a friendly,

Written by Trisha Amable – Girlfridayz – Website: https://girlfridayz.com
Girllfridayz number 10358020 girlfriday, girlfridayz[tm] is a registered trademark in the UK

solution-oriented professional manner than having a robot doing that which is annoying for prospects and customers resulting in lost sales or new customer acquisition.

What you should be using instead is the telephone to communicate with your prospect or customers about products or services and answer more specific questions. Also, using a telemarketing strategy allows for a more personalised conversation and allows you to gather more information from a potential customer or customers if your answer is provided in a friendly soft tone of voice, polite, friendly, professional and answer the receiver pain point and satisfy a need.

How to address customers' needs when you do not have the product or service sighted

When you have a customer or potential customer that has a specific need for a product, however, in your shop or online store you do not have the product wanted, but you may have a similar product to offer that can potentially answer their needs, you should attempt to secure a sale by offering the similar products instead. However, if you do not have anything at all that can match the need identified you can secure future referrals by using the B2B referral strategy.

You can refer your prospect or customers to your direct competitor or indirect competitor that can answer the need of the prospect or your customer. You are not losing anything but in the long run, you will be gaining sales.

By working in collaboration with your competitor and not rivalry you are satisfying the customer's or prospect's need because your competitor may have in stock the product that your prospect or customer requires. Or if you are a services company your competitor may be able to provide the service that the customer requires.

The B2B referral strategy provides benefits to both companies. It is a win-win strategy because the prospect or customer in turn may refer your business to their friends, family, associate or even a stranger during an innocent conversation because of the support receive during their query about the product or service needed at the time. The consumer appreciates greatly the gesture and remembers the company that has helped them satisfy their needs.

Your competitor, in turn, can refer their prospects or customers to you if they cannot satisfy their needs and knows that your company can in essence pay forward a return the favour.

An example of this strategy and how it works wonderfully to answer my need.

I needed to change the chain set of my Giant CSR bicycle due to wear and tear because it has never been replaced since I purchased my bicycle in 2006.

After a discussion with my friend about which bicycle shop, I should go to; he recommended Halford because they are a large business, but also told me I could go to Edwardes a small family business owner that you always went to. I replied that I shall go to Halford they are in Brixton closer to me.

Written by Trisha Amable – Girlfridayz – Website: https://girlfridayz.com
Girllfridayz number 10358020 girlfriday, girlfridayz™ is a registered trademark in the UK

The next day I went to Halford in Brixton and spoke to a member of staff. I informed him that my bicycle is 16 years old, and its chain set needed replacing. I added that I have purchased the replacement chain set with a chain guard and if they could fit it for me.

The staff replied you looked after it well after looking at my bicycle. I replied thank you, but can you fit the new chain set. He replied no they are fully booked for a month or so and I would have to wait. I replied I don't mind the wait it is not an urgent job, I added I would have done it myself, but I don't know how to do it. He replied wait here a minute, I am going to ask my manager if we can replace your chain set. He went to ask his manager and return after several minutes saying sorry my manager said that we don't replace chain sets it is a technical job and we don't have the staff.

The staff carried on saying we tend to change brakes, and pedals that is what we do. I replied do you know another bicycle shop that can fit my bicycle chain set? He replied, Brixton Cycle, I am sure they can do it for you. He then looked at his phone and give me the direction and location of Brixton Cycle. He added at Brixton Cycle they have technical staff who can do this job for you.

I replied thank I will make my way there. I thought the staff was informative and helpful, he referred me to an independent small business that has expert staff in bicycle repair. I made my way there and on arrival, I waited a bit before getting served.

A staff member approached me and said hello "what seems to be the problem" with my bicycle. I informed him that I have my Giant CRS bicycle for 16 years and the original chain set had never been changed in 16 years. He replied you looked after it well. I replied, yes; it is my ride, I don't have a car.

He checked my bicycle and asked specific questions about the chain set. He initially stated there is nothing wrong with it. I replied yes there is and elaborated that when I ride on a flat road it feels like riding on the hill leading to the Blackwall tunnel in East London and I have pain in my upper leg up to my knee.

He replied your knee hurt it might be the chain set or your fitness and quickly added I ride every day and sometimes I feel exhausted. I replied you say you feel exhausted because you ride daily, I replied this is different than me having pain in my upper leg going to my knee. It is the chain set it is very old and has wear and tear. He replied after looking closely at my chain set "you tend to ride on the 8 speeds, the first chain ring and sometimes on the second but rarely on the third chain ring because it is not torn it looks fine".

I replied I know but it is a set and I have purchased the Giant CRS chain Shimano chain sets replacement can you fit in or not? He replied oh course I can, and I will do what the customer requires and added you bought the right one too and a Shimano too. I replied I repurchased the original chain set which came with my bicycle when I purchased it. I researched it and found the online store that sells it.

I added how much will it cost me for you to fit it. He replied £15 for the fitting as you supplied the part. I replied do you have a new seat too because as you can see my seat and the seat

145

cover are wormed out and hurt my bottom. He replied yes, I have one and went to fetch it for me. He said this seat will fit neatly on your Giant CSR Bicycle and it cost £25. I replied that's fine and how much is the total bill, please. He replied £39 and you can pay for the collection of your bicycle, I will send you a text message when it's ready to collect. I replied thank you, but I prefer to pay you today. He took the card payment and issued me a receipt that said paid zero due.

I collected my bicycle from Brixton Cycle within three days. My bicycle is new now after testing it on my way back home. I further tested it when going to do exercise and a short, long warm-up ride, my bicycle felt roadworthy and like a brand-new bicycle.

The customer service experience at Brixton Cycle was top and the staff who fitted my new chain set and the new seat on my Giant CRS bicycle had the right technical skills for the job.

Due to the good customer service, I have received from Brixton Cycle, I would be more likely to return to use their services or purchase bicycle equipment when I need it.

Here's what happened when a small family business ensures longevity

Business longevity is the ability of a business to survive through time. Business owners who achieve exceptional business success think differently about their business, their goals, and long-term success. They tend to be realistic about what they can do, disciplined, consistent, customer-centric, adaptable, build business control and maintain their success through the years despite the struggle a business may face and must overcome to remain sustainable.

Most business owners dream of passing it along to their family or trusted colleagues or the next generation. However, a few businesses succeed in sustaining their business through time.

Every year, countless small businesses fail, close, or sell out to their competitor their business model because they cannot envisage themselves in the future or to a successor who shares their vision. Most of the time when a business fails, excuses are made or finger-pointing, as well as blaming someone else or something else for their failure except taking accountability or responsibility for their failure.

Long-term business success takes more than hard work and a little luck. The business owner who achieves exceptional success and longevity through time shares 8 business practices that guide them to long-term success and longevity.

They tend to think differently and operate differently than the norm. These are the techniques that help them make the transition to the next generation of successful leaders, entrepreneurs, and long-term successful small business owners.

1. **Engage in ongoing planning with a realistic vision** – meaning they are disciplined in the habit of writing down their plans, reviewing them, and sharing them with their essential employees and advisors. They know that ongoing planning keeps them

Written by Trisha Amable – Girlfridayz – Website: https://girlfridayz.com
Girllfridayz number 10358020 girlfriday, girlfridayz™ is a registered trademark in the UK

moving forward. These business owners continually and formally, evaluate what is working and what needs to be changed or discontinued.

2. **Establish a realistic vision** – Lasting business owners match their vision to their abilities, skills, and knowledge. They leverage one success into another rather than making rapids huge leap beyond their capabilities. Enduring business owners actively and effectively manage their transitions and hire sophisticated talent to match their future needs. Their success is sustainable because it is built on viable foundations that are based on strong thinking and not on wishful thinking.

3. **Use disciplined approaches to developing leadership and executive skills** – Business owners who understand, experience, critics and struggle are necessary for growth, not just operational and technical expertise. They can lead, manage and weather the daily challenges of not having someone tell you what to do. These business owners understand they need to continue cultivating their abilities to manage and create strategies and system thinking in their business. The business owners with enduring success continue developing their skills to expand their resources, grow their opportunities and build their business arsenal. They read they hire consulting and professional talent they need to increase their internal expertise.

4. **Implement sound financial management** – Financial management is fundamental to long-term business success. Therefore, successful leaders of enduring businesses focus on building net worth and assets by mastering financial discipline and tightly controlling spending.

5. **Adapt to changing circumstances** – Market change and technological advancement require a business to adapt. Successful business owners who remain for years to come understand and adapt to change. They invest in people and technology to enhance productivity. They stay on top of the competition and respond as necessary. By moving with their time, they can leverage emerging trends and long-term evolutions that are fundamentally transforming their industries. Long-term business owners create businesses that last well beyond their tenure, always looking ahead to identify tools, resources, ideas, and technology that can enhance their business success.

6. **Building substance into their business** – Sustainable businesses have substance. They deliver on promises they make, and fulfil the expectation they raise, with their customers, suppliers, and employees who can count on them. These businesses demonstrate a consistency of quality products or services that can be trusted over time. An ongoing reputation for dependability is often a predictor of long-term business success.

7. **Control growth** – Business owners that survive over the years have leaders who carefully and deliberately manage the size of their business. These business owners

Written by Trisha Amable – Girlfridayz – Website: https://girlfridayz.com
Girllfridayz number 10358020 girlfriday, girlfridayz[tm] is a registered trademark in the UK

focus on growth ensuring that the business has adequate finances, equipment, and staff to meet their evolving needs. Those business owners who maintain a smaller size often find they are better at managing the stability of their overhead and fixed costs. Maintenance-oriented businesses may even make more money and have less stress than their growth-oriented peers. Both growth and maintenance-oriented business owners who succeed throughout times effectively manage their appetite for risk and keep the scope of their business within their comfort zone. They maintain leadership enthusiasm and motivation by controlling the pace of growth or by achieving sustained financial success.

8. **Maintain motivation** – Business owners of enduring businesses motivate themselves and their employees by continuing to look for new opportunities to meet their customers' needs. This creates an atmosphere of innovation and ongoing success measured in revenues, customer satisfaction, and employee retention. Businesses that enjoy enduring success have learned to constantly adapt and evolve. They respond to continuing competitive pressures by finding ways to meet evolving client needs.

The secret to longevity in business sustainable success is to do things with discipline, consistency, grit, and excellence. In essence, successful business owners make their success a reality by taking the actions necessary to achieve it and to make it last.

Are you ready to be a leader of an enduring company like Edwardes?

Here's an example of a customer using Edwardes a family small business for over 20 years.

In hindsight thinking about a small family business Edwardes a bicycle shop in Camberwell and I became a regular customer for over 20 years, it is because over the years they provided friendly, professional, consistent, customer-centric services to me since I set foot in their shop to purchase my first bicycle.

I stayed that long, and they became top of mind it is because of the consistent expert friendly service received by the owner and the staff team over the years no change in service provision and the front of the shop staff (The sales team). Therefore, Edwardes has not become complacent over the years and got it right and embodied the attitude and approach of enduring business owners motivating themselves and their employees by continuing to look for new opportunities to meet their customers' needs achieving business profitability and longevity.

Meaning that Edwardes is a customer-centric business that put its customers' needs first and answer their pain point to perfection because when one of my very expensive high-quality Giant CRS 9 speeds bicycle purchases got stolen 2 days after collection, Edwardes was there for me.

Replaced Bike

Edwardes owner used the sympathy strategy when I called the shop to inform them that my bicycle got stolen within two days of collecting it from their shop.

How Edwardes used the Sympathy strategy to answer my pain

Here is the deal used by Edwardes owner. I was distraught and hurt when my Giant CRS Black 9 speeds bicycle got lifted in front of my face. I was at work and the thief looked at my bicycle tied up to the railing. He stared at it for some time in admiration and left.

He shortly returned with a pair of bolt cutters and cut my cheap bicycle lock in two, then jumped on my bicycle seat and start riding. I came out of the office and ran after him but could not catch up with him. He was too fast, and the cut lock was trailing behind, he outruns me in no time.

I contacted Edwardes over the phone, and I was emotional. The owner listened to me when I told him exactly this.

"My Giant bicycle {product} just got stolen in front of my face, I was at work and the thief used bolt cutters to cut my lock, I could not catch up with him and saw him riding away with my bicycle. I am still paying for it. I have £250 left on it; due next month." {customer distraught}

"He replied I am so sorry in a concerned voice and continue saying have you reported it to the police?" {owner show concern but kept it professional}

"I replied yes, I have, and they are asking for the bicycle serial number. I could not give it to them. I don't even know where to find it and my bicycle got stolen." {customer requesting info based on the police report)

"He replied I am ever so sorry for your lost, but it is not our responsibility Trisha {inbound strategy}, we cannot give you another bicycle for free as a replacement because it is not our fault." (owner stressed that he is concerned and introduced a replacement product}

"I replied I was not calling for you to give me another bicycle, {Power word use repeated} but for the serial number of my Giant CRS {the product} for the police."

{Sale speech} "He replied I am afraid we don't have it on record. Do you want another bicycle Trisha {inbound strategy}, we have in a store another Giant CRS Blue 8 speeds the model slightly under your previous bicycle. {New product introduced} It has 1 speed less, but it is the same high-quality Trisha, {inbound strategy} the frame is light and the wheel too. {FB} The difference between the two models is minimal." {D}

"I replied yes, but I owe you £250 left on my stolen bicycle payable next month. I paid £549 already. How much is the new Giant please?" {customer sold}

{The deal} "He replied, the Giant CRS 8 speeds Blue cost £699, however, what I can do for you Trisha {inbound strategy} is I will transfer your payment of £549 to the new bicycle and you will only have to pay £250 remaining next month {IO}. Would you like to purchase the Giant CRS Blue 7 speeds, Trisha?" {gentle persuasion} {CTA}

149

Written by Trisha Amable – Girlfridayz – Website: https://girlfridayz.com
Girllfridayz number 10358020 girlfriday, girlfridayz^{tm} is a registered trademark in the UK

"I replied yes, I am very grateful for the offer, thank you very much, you are ever so kind and agreed." {customer agreement}

"He replied come and collect it on Saturday, It's a brand-new bicycle and it will be ready for you by the weekend Trisha." {Customer delivery confirmation} {customer happy}

When I collected my new bicycle pictured (p.144) the Blue Giant 8 speeds CRS Bicycle, I also purchase two strong chain locks for each wheel each £50. {related Item purchase on the spot} I thought that if someone want to steal my bicycle again they would have a hard time cutting through these locks. It also taught me to never put a cheap lock on an expensive bicycle.

How I became a long-term customer of Edwardes and referred other people to them

The offer Edwardes did for me when I was despondent {customer pain answer and needs met} kept me returning to the shop to purchase equipment and repair my bicycle as well as monthly MOT because I used it every day to go to work for several years before starting virtualgirlfridayz.co.uk my own online business.

It's because Edwardes uphold excellent professional, friendly customer service consistently over the years. He ensured that their customers return to use their services, purchase a bicycle for all ages at varied prices, or upgraded bicycles and equipment and accessories by moving with their times and always keeping a professional, friendly, informative approach as well as always demonstrating their expertise by answering competently all their customer's questions about bicycles, equipment, clothing, and accessories. Therefore, every time someone asked about a bicycle shop for their bicycle, the first business name that came to mind was Edwardes.

How Edwardes used the Nostalgia Strategy and it failed

When working for One Housing Group in Garett Lane Tooting, my Giant CRS Blue Bicycle needed fixing and I rode from work to Edwardes. I wheeled my bicycle into the shop and waited a bit then the owners came to me.

"The owner said what seem to be the problem. Trisha" {inbound strategy}

"I replied, my bicycle brake has an issue, and the wheel feels flat", {customer problem} "He checked my bicycle and noticed the brake was wormed out and he added you may have a hole in your inner tube." {diagnosing issue} "He replied, put your bike by the counter and one staff will check the wheel".

"He added it is a long time Trisha you have not purchased a new bicycle, {Nostalgia Strategy} we have in-store new models, would you like to have a look."

"I replied why not while I am waiting for my ticket for my repair." {Customer compliance}

150

Written by Trisha Amable – Girlfridayz – Website: https://girlfridayz.com
Girllfridayz number 10358020 girlfriday, girlfridayz^{tm} is a registered trademark in the UK

"I went around the store and look at all the bicycles suitable for me, however, I did not find any suitable ones. He did not have any Giant bicycles in store, and he had more expensive bikes as a new arrival. I was not interested in any of them because the shape of the frame was different from my bicycle."

"He asked me did you see anything that you like Trisha, {inbound strategy} we have new arrivals and some of them are being mounted but some are ready."

"I replied not interested I like the shape of my bicycle – the frame it's nice and suitable for me." {strategy failed}

"He replied never mind another time may be. We going to take your bike in, here's your ticket that will cost £50 for the labour, change of brakes, and burst inner tube, you have a tiny hole in them there is a pin stocked in the tire done it."

"I replied cash or card, I can pay by cash or card today.", "He replied card and asked a staff to take the payment and went to attend to another customer."

"The staff took the payment and told me to collect my bicycle in 7 days."

Why did the Nostalgia Strategy fail on this occasion?

It's because I love my Giant replacement bicycle, it's in terms of bicycle speed when riding and the lightness of the frame at maximum speed is minimal, you can still go fast with an eight speeds high-quality bicycle and it was fast when roadworthy, therefore, why replace it, nothing wrong with it and it served its purpose.

Why I have temporarily left Edwardes and went to Harbour Cycle in Camberwell

In 2020 my Giant CRS Bicycle was 14 years old, and I brought it for an MOT at Edwardes, the owner was not in, and the staff attended to my bicycle. I told him that I needed an MOT done and my bicycle was slow.

He replied that to leave it at the counter and it will cost you £65 for the check-up. I replied that fine and paid the fee. On collection of my bicycle a week after the original spiky pedal was changed to flat pedals.

I collected my Giant CRS and the staff told me that they changed my chain, pumped my tires, and changed my pedals. The brake was fine, and the chain set and speed cassette were fine.

I replied, my pedals did not have any issues and I never told you to change them, I want my old pedals back. The staff attending to me said on the ticket it says changed pedals. I replied it is not my ticket and showed my ticket that only said, checked up £65.

He called the owner and said Trisha is asking why her pedal have been changed. He checked the ticket and noticed that it was not written the change pedals. He informed me that it is a

Written by Trisha Amable – Girlfridayz – Website: https://girlfridayz.com
Girllfridayz number 10358020 girlfriday, girlfridayz[tm] is a registered trademark in the UK

misunderstanding, and the new pedals are nice, my spike pedals started to be wormed out, hence we replaced them.

I replied thank you, but I did not ask you to do this for me. I would like my spike pedal back. He replied, Trisha I am afraid we have disposed of them; therefore, we cannot put them back for you.

I replied ok, I have already paid for the job and left with my Giant CRS Bicycle home and when it next checked up was due, I used Harbour Cycle.

You see I left because they did not do what the customer asked and changed my pedals, If they were to change my pedals part of the check-up they should have informed me, and I could have made an informed decision.

However, no one told me that parts may be replaced as part of the check-up or we will replace any parts we noticed worn out or broken and discuss this with you before repairing.

In terms of customer acquisition and retention, you must ensure that you always do what the customers request or expect of your business. If the customer is not happy they will leave for your competitor and not give you a good review depending on the severity of the issues or mistake or do not place a review at all but stop using your business together and tell their peer about why they left.

Word of the wise: **Ensure that you always do what the customers requested** and expect from your company as well as **ensure you have an SLA (service level agreement) or other contractual documentation, to protect your business against unscrupulous customers too.**

In November 2021 I visited Harbour Cycle in Camberwell to change the chain set {The part that needed replacement} of my Giant 8 speeds CSR blue Bicycle {the product}. It was the original chain set never been changed since I purchased it in 2006 (my bicycle was 15 years old).

"The owner asked how I can help you Trisha, tu vas bien?" {owner knows the customer}

"I replied, je vais bien, and you?", "He replied, I 'm fine, what's wrong with your bicycle?"

"I replied, my chain set needs replacing it has never been replaced since I bought it a couple of years back." {customer informed the owner of the problem}

"He replied, it's going to be expensive and start totalling the price of the chain set, then checked my bicycle and said the speed cassette need to be replaced, the chain and the brakes."

"I replied, my chain is fine, how much for the job." "He replied £154 for the parts and the labour".

"I replied, can I pay £89 now and the rest on collections?" "He replied, yes, and presented his card reader and I paid £89, he said collects it on Saturday, and issued a receipt detailing the job to be done (the chain set, the chain, the cassette, the brakes) and remaining amount £65".

A week later I visited Harbour Cycle to collect my bicycle.

"The owner said it is ready Trisha you owe me £65; how do you want to settle the remaining amount of £65." {payment request first again}

"I replied card and where is my bicycle I don't see it?" "Wait a minute, I get it for you let me take the payment first and presented his card reader." {The customer is concerned about the product}

I paid £65 and said "Can you go and get my bicycle, please; I need to check it" he went and get it and give it to me. {customer requested her bike}

After checking thoroughly, I said:

"You have not changed the chain set as requested and you charged me for it, I have a new chain, new brakes and new 8 speeds cassette, however, the chain was fine as you told me in January 2021 when you changed it to a secondhand chain from another bicycle without my permission when I brought my bicycle for a check-up. {The customer confronts the owner about previous dishonesty}

However, if you remember I told you that you replaced my chain changed by Edwardes last year with a secondhand chain."

"He replied, Trisha you have a new bicycle now, I have not changed the chain set because there is nothing wrong with it, and your chain needed replacement, as well as your speed cassette and your tires, are a bit worm look at them, Trisha." {owner denial}

He showed me my front tire that had a bit of tear but nothing major, the secondhand tire that he replaced in January 2021 because the original was wormed out. "He added he could not get some parts and he did not charge me enough" {diminish responsibility}

"I replied, I don't think so, you owe me a refund you have not replaced the chain set as requested and it is on you if you did not charge me enough, not on me. Also, you are dishonest because you trying to get more money out of me, and you did not change the chain set as requested but I have been charged for it."

"He replied just test your bicycle outside Trisha the money is fine thank you for using me." {owner denial} "I replied, bye and it is the last time I support your small business, and you better be careful some customers might not be as nice as me letting you off with their money for a job not done."

Written by Trisha Amable – Girlfridayz – Website: https://girlfridayz.com
Girllfridayz number 10358020 girlfriday, girlfridayz^{tm} is a registered trademark in the UK

The owner was ashamed because he knew me for years in the area, and he knew full well that the neighbouring shop Mana Jai the owner was my friend and I visited them often. He was afraid that I start telling my friend that he defrauded me and lost business.

In January 2021 I went to Edwardes and asked them if they could change my front and back tires.

Edwardes owner was happy to see me and said we have not seen you in a long time, Trisha, how have you been? I replied fine, just busy running my own company now. The owners and the front staff said Wow well done, what do you do? I replied I run an online marketing and business support company Girlfridayz Limited and offered my business card.

The owner took my business card and said Girlfridayz is your business for women. I replied no unisex and how much for both tires. He replied, £30 each, I said that fine and settled £60 for my tires to be changed.

He replied thank you and come to collect your bicycle on Monday evening it will be ready for you Trisha. I replied fine see you on Monday. When I collected my bicycle I had two new tires.

Excellent Customer Service is important for client retention and business longevity

Have you noticed the difference in customer service from both small businesses in the same cycling industry? Both owners have a clear different approaches when it comes to customer service.

Edwardes has previously stated is a business customer-centric and know the foundation of marketing and its application to business. The owner mastered the marketing skills and learned to sell without selling; view the technic and expertise in marketing at play (p.144). Edwardes's ethics and business image are professional and friendly, and the customers come first. It shows in their customer service and the longevity of their family small business.

On the other hand, Harbour Cycle is not customer-centric and overall, their small business ethic and business image are based on dishonesty and money oriented before the customer's welfare and needs or pain. This is demonstrated by not carried work requested by me the customer and not meeting my need. He did not provide me with a solution but tried to defraud me by asking for more money and never issued me with a refund for the chain set part of my bicycle paid in advance that he never got.

When confronted he denied the allegations and try to distract me with other information, the owner lack of accountability and responsibility for his action as he run his business on his own with one occasional part-time seasonal staff coming to help with his partner on occasion.

Customer service is in your business the provision of services to customers before, during, and after a purchase. Customer service is very important in your business it can make or break your business. It is an important part of the value chain of clients. Each industry requires

Written by Trisha Amable – Girlfridayz – Website: https://girlfridayz.com
Girllfridayz number 10358020 girlfriday, girlfridayz^tm is a registered trademark in the UK

different levels of customer service. However, the concept of a well-performed service is that of increasing revenues. Essentially, the 3 important qualities of customer service are centred around three "p" s: Professionalism, Patience, and a people-first attitude.

Although customer service varies from customer to customer, if you're following the 3ps of customer service you're on the right track and must always keep it professional. Great customer service means following best practices like:

- Valuing customers' time
- Having a pleasant attitude
- Be knowledgeable
- Knowing your products or services
- Maintain a positive attitude
- Creatively solve problem
- Respond quickly
- Personalize services
- Help customers help themselves
- Focus support on customers
- Actively listen
- Keep your word (do what you say you will do)
- Be proactively helpful

Customer service is mighty important for business survival in any industry, and you must always demonstrate your expertise to your customers and give them resourceful resources but ensure that you take a step further to exceed – rather than just meet customers' expectations.

Without excellent customer service, your customer will gravitate towards your competitors and will give your business a bad reputation, by posting on social media their bad experience and depending on your response to a complaint it might go viral in a negative manner for you. However, if you provide excellent customer service your customer will rewards you and post a review recommending you every chance they get and signing your praise likewise it can go viral in a positive way and your customer database increase greatly as well as your revenue and business profitability, retention, and longevity. You might become top of mind meaning instant word-of-mouth referral.

The Offer

Celebrate with us our 7 years in business readers of this playbook. We are offering you an opportunity to join us in the 7 figures Book Drive, however, readers I can't promise you you'll make 7 figures, obviously, but I guarantee if you read a business or marketing book you'll soak up the knowledge and implement the knowledge you'll be part of the 7 figures small business community.

Reading Marketing, Business books, instead of getting 4000 clients per year, you'll be getting 15000 clients per year and you'll be part of the biggest Book Drive worldwide...I 'am building

Written by Trisha Amable – Girlfridayz – Website: https://girlfridayz.com
Girllfridayz number 10358020 girlfriday, girlfridayz[tm] is a registered trademark in the UK

a small business community of book readers and I want you to be part of it and join the latest craze of small business owners getting the knowledge and using it in their business to make 7 figures in less than 7 years just by implementing what learned. We're building the finest small business community, and the readers have full access to the mentoring system attached to this Playbook – The Cellar and we want you to be part of it.

Plus, I have assembled what I believe to be the best and most unique Mentoring Support System – The Cellar attached to this book to support business owners who join us in Celebrating our 7 years in business milestone and joining the largest Book Drive that the world has seen.

I have put all this in place to ensure business owners become better at marketing their business to the right audience for their industries and I don't believe you'll get that level of training and support anywhere else.

At Girlfridayz we're ahead of everyone else. I have put the steps in place to create a professional, world-class structure which is unmatched anywhere else where small business owners can thrive, learn, improve, and grow their business by acquiring skills, knowledge and abilities by learning progressive methodology in Marketing and its application to business and it is ready for you to join because you'll be part of the winning league of small business owners achieving massive success and longevity.

I hope you've enjoyed reading the playbook (The Manual) and taken in the knowledge so far. I appreciate you may feel overwhelmed now, but 7 figures are in your grasp if you apply a fraction of what I've revealed to you in this book, you'll be on your way to creating a successful 7 figures small business in any industry.

However, in all my 7 years of supporting and helping many hundreds of small businesses with our services and standalone services and encouraging them to thrive. It may surprise you to know there is ONE BIG PROBLEM which holds most back.

They don't have the resources, time, and money to put everything in place for each of the 7 elements. However, for you to get to this point; reading this book, you can, of course, do it, but it will take a considerable effort, time, and investment.

But there is a low-cost and less time-intensive solution... It's called THE CELLAR attached to this book. I have taken everything detailed in this book (and much more) to create the world's first largest and most successful small business community accessing the Mentoring Support System attached to this Playbook.

The Cellar comes with everything you need to start building and scaling a world-class 7 figures small business. However, with ZERO up-front licences or training fees and no exorbitant monthly support fees, you can have the entire Mentoring Support System for a quarterly one-time fee or a 6-month fee because you can purchase 3 months or 6 months of use of The Cellar Membership Support System for your small business the complete solution for building and scaling your small business to 7 figures should you implement the system content.

156

Written by Trisha Amable – Girlfridayz – Website: https://girlfridayz.com
Girllfridayz number 10358020 girlfriday, girlfridayz[tm] is a registered trademark in the UK

CELEBRATING GIRLFRIDAYZ 7 YEARS IN BUSINESS IS OUR SIGNIFICANT MILESTONE.

5 Signs of a Marketing Book Lover

Book Drive

1

When you open a book, you soak up knowledge

2

Your dreams are about "Book Drive", and using the knowledge

3

You LOVE a hot bath because you can relax with a good book in your hands.

4

Your dream office includes shelves filled with your favourite business book oozing knowledge

5

You always believe reading books increase revenue and profitability

**YOU KNOW!
THE LOVE OF BOOKS IS GREAT
FOR SELF-DEVELOPMENT
AND MENTAL HEALTH.**

Read more about great business and marketing books at
girlfridayz.com/online-store

157

Written by Trisha Amable – Girlfridayz – Website: https://girlfridayz.com
Girllfridayz number 10358020 girlfriday, girlfridayz^{tm} is a registered trademark in the UK

Marketing Essential from Girlfridayz Limited Online Marketing and Business Support Consultancy Cie

The concept behind The Core Assets of Marketing With Its Dual Implementation Support System – The Cellar is that the postgraduate and undergraduate students will learn the foundation of marketing, digital and traditional marketing including theoretical innovative intangible strategical matrices and analysis business models.

The Playbook with its attached online Mentoring Business Support System – The Cellar is compatible with any classroom Digital Marketing course offered by Universities because it offers a possibility for the students to access internship and work in an organisation to gain work-based learning, practical experience or satisfy the requirement for qualification.

Students love Girlfridayz Limited because they produce results. Each year, hundreds of thousands of students improve their test scores and final grades with these indispensable legacy system study guides. Master essential Marketing Strategies and Tactics with Girlfridayz Marketing Consultancy and Business Support online company—the high-performance legacy system study guides, to help you to cut study time, hone problem-solving, and achieve your personal best on exams!

Students need to read the book first and learn the foundation of marketing (digital & traditional marketing including theoretical strategic business models) before accessing the cellar for further practical material and strategies and tactics they will get the access passcode of the Cellar that is inside the book. They therefore cannot get access to the Cellar without reading the Marketing Playbook first.

Our innovation purpose comes from answering one question "most people do not implement what learn in their business and complain of very little sales" after pondering on this question we developed our Marketing Playbook and attached a Dual Steps by Steps mentoring implementation support system to it. It is the first Marketing book attached to an online implementation step-by-step mentoring support system and we are very proud of our achievement.

Girlfridayz Limited Online Marketing Consultancy company give you the information teachers expect you to know in a handy and succinct format —without overwhelming you with unnecessary details and covers the entire course Digital Marketing course—theory, definitions, problems and more.

- The perfect aid for better grades!
- Can be used alone or with a group class or with any class text
- Saves study time
- Achieve 70% internship apprenticeship learning and 30% career and personal development plan completed and ready for a post in their desired company or remaining working for their internship if any vacancies are available and like the employers.

158

Written by Trisha Amable – Girlfridayz – Website: https://girlfridayz.com
Girllfridayz number 10358020 girlfriday, girlfridayz™ is a registered trademark in the UK

- Brush up before tests
- Find answers fast
- Study quickly and more effectively
- Get the big picture without spending hours poring over lengthy textbooks

You get a complete Marketing dual step-by-step implementation Mentoring business Support System of the subject marketing and its application to business. Plus, you get The Cellar which gives you plenty of practice exercises to test your skills. The Marketing Support system lets you study at your own pace and reminds you of all important progressive Strategies and Tactics, facts you need to remember—fast! And Girlfridayz's online Marketing and Business Consultancy company The Core Assets of Marketing With Its Dual Implementation Support System are complete, they're perfect for preparing postgraduate and undergraduate for qualifications or professional exams.

If you want top grades and an understanding of Marketing and Its Application to Business, this powerful study tool is the best tutor you can have!

Get the edge on your Classmates! Use The Core Assets Of Marketing With Its Dual Implementation Support System – The Cellar.

This book is available in two formats – Paperback version on Amazon (UK, CA, FR, COM...) and as an E-Books version that you can purchase from our store and purchase the Cellar from our Store 3 months Cellar use or 6 months Cellar use payable quarterly in one lump sum online.

Students can evidence their learning using the fill-in-the-blank found in the Cellar and incorporate their findings from the subject matter and gain a more complete, intuitive understanding of the concept of self-reflection through writing their thought in a learning journal which is important for personal development and personal growth as well as anything you desire to innovate and create then develop.

The Core Assets of Marketing With Its Dual Implementation Support System – The Cellar makes the student's problem solving easier, with powerful templates, and quickly does a wide range of marketing technical tasks. All formulas needed to solve prospects and customers' problems in real time appears in the Marketing methodology and technics used in this book to help you think in your head to generate solution-oriented for your future prospective customers and customers.

The cellar interactive Online Mentoring Implementation Business Support System uses a wide range of built-in functions, units, and graphics features branded in an easy funny attractive package making learning the subject matter easier, more effective, and even fun.

Pick a book with substances, patronage intention and related topics designed for students, educators and technical professionals in Marketing and Its Application to Business. New format available Hardcover if you prefer strudier cover to hold in your hands.

Written by Trisha Amable – Girlfridayz – Website: https://girlfridayz.com
Girllfridayz number 10358020 girlfriday, girlfridayz[tm] is a registered trademark in the UK

The Cellar Membership
What you're going to get...

- Open your ears & Open your eyes value £590
- Sale enabler accelerator fill-in-the-blank templates value £696
- The wine vault mapped out templates value £794
- My Personal Support value £29.20 PM

Total Cellar Membership Value £2906.20

The Core Assets of Marketing
What you're going to get...

- Sale Acquisition **Book Price £67.97**
- Lead Attraction
- Increase traffic to your website
- Methodologic pre-design templates
- Marketing Models
- Audience Attraction
- Customer Acquisition & Retention
- The Core Assets & how to combine them with strategies

+

Total value of the Dual Implementation Support System £2974.17

Get Started After Reading
FOR JUST
£242.20 PER MONTH
payable quarterly

Read It today
FOR JUST
£67.97 FOR LIFE

GET IT NOW: INCREASE YOUR REACH

160

Printed by Amazon Italia Logistica S.r.l.
Torrazza Piemonte (TO), Italy

46689749R00092